KT-449-608

FAIR ISLE
AN ISLAND SAGA

FAIR ISLE
AN ISLAND SAGA

Valerie M. Thom

JOHN DONALD PUBLISHERS LTD
EDINBURGH

© Valerie M. Thom 1989

All rights reserved. No part of this publication may be
reproduced in any form or by any means without the
prior permission of the publishers,
John Donald Publishers Ltd.,
138 St Stephen Street
Edinburgh EH3 5AA

ISBN 0 85976 250 5
The publishers acknowledge the financial assistance of
the Scottish Arts Council in the publication of
this volume.

Phototypeset by Pioneer Associates Ltd., Perthshire
Printed in Great Britain by
Bell & Bain Ltd., Glasgow.

Preface

Almost from the time of his first visit to the island, George Waterston had plans for a book about Fair Isle, and over 40 years he gradually amassed records of island life, past and present, including scrapbooks of news-cuttings, boxes of photographs, and an extensive bibliography. Some of this material appeared in his posthumous FAIR ISLE — A photographic history', and several chapters of a more comprehensive book had been drafted by his wife Irene before she died in 1984. All this material was left to Fair Isle Bird Observatory Trust, of which I am currently Honorary Secretary. Having myself been a 'Fair Isle addict' for many years, I decided to take up the task which the Waterstons had been unable to complete, and try to produce a book which would reflect not only the history and natural history of the island but also the changing patterns of its community life.

Spelling presents particular problems in a book of this kind. As a result of progressive anglicisation of Norse place-names, and attempts at phonetic representation of dialect words, many different versions of the same word may exist, and it is not possible to say which is 'the correct one'. For example, 'yole' and 'yoal' are both widely used, and 'Claver (or Klaver) Geo' are alternatives to 'Geo Claver'. In making somewhat arbitrary choices I have endeavoured (except when quoting from other people's writings) to stick to what seem to me the most acceptable spellings, but I appreciate that not everyone will agree with my choice.

In the course of writing this book I have been helped by many different people, and in many different ways; I offer my thanks to them all. Brian Smith, Shetland Archivist, and Alan Perkins of the Northern Lighthouse Board directed me to valuable contemporary accounts of 19th century developments, and Donald Erskine of the National Trust for Scotland gave me access to NTS Fair Isle files covering the last 45 years. William Waterston kindly lent me his father's diaries, several of George's friends provided reminiscences of early visits to the isle, and such diverse bodies as the Queen's Nursing Institute, Coats of Paisley, and Lloyds of London responded helpfully to my enquiries. Specialist comment on the natural history chapters was willingly given by Paul Harvey, Mike Richardson, Nick Riddiford, Walter Scott and Peter Slater, and on archaeological matters by John Hunter and Val Turner. I am grateful for all the help given by the islanders, and am especially indebted to Anne Sinclair and Alec Stout, who read and commented on drafts of nearly all the chapters. Finally, I wish to thank my good friends Joe Eggeling and Roberta Seath, who have done their best to ensure that the book will be readable and also intelligible to those who are not lucky enough to know Fair Isle.

I should like to think that the outcome of my efforts to complete this task would have pleased George and Irene, and I certainly hope that it will encourage readers to visit Fair Isle and see it for themselves. There is far more to the Fair Isle story than can possibly be encompassed in one small book.

For permission to reproduce illustrations in the colour section, I would like to thank Alexander Bennett (pages 2 (bottom), 3 (top), 4 (bottom), 5 (bottom right), 6, 7 (top) and 8 (top)); and the National Trust for Scotland (pages 3 (bottom) and 5 (top and bottom left)).

Black & white photo credits (references are to page numbers): Aerofilms 2, 9; Roger Broad 115; Dennis Coutts 103, 107; Roy Dennis 38; Royal Commission on Ancient & Historical Monuments/R. Lamb 11; George Waterston Memorial Centre 20, 76, 79, 85; George Waterston Collection 24, 25, 27, 29, 33, 45, 47, 50, 55, 59, 60, 67, 69, 101 & 119; National Trust for Scotland 13, 43, 74, 94; William S. Paton 131; Popperfoto 98; Scottish Ethnological Archive, National Museums of Scotland 35, 58, 81, 113; Pat Sellar 57; Shetland Museum 83; John Topham Picture Library 4; The Trustees of the Imperial War Museum, London 92; Trustees of the Science Museum (London) 31; Dave Wheeler 7, 18, 23, 41, 63, 64, 73, 87, 90, 96, 105, 129, 135, 137, 138, 141; The author 37, 123, 127.

The poems on page 71 are reproduced by permission of John Graham (1 & 2) and the Estate of John Betjeman.

Contents

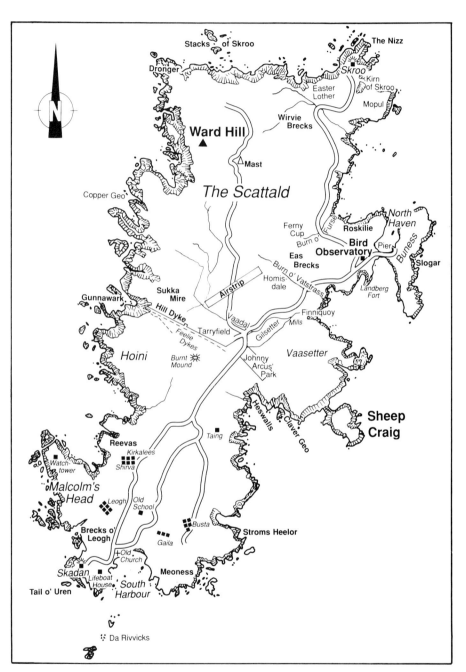

Map 1 shows most of the physical features mentioned in the text, also the
locations of the 19th-century townships, the old church and the old school.
Although the present road system did not exist when the townships were
occupied, it is included to assist orientation. The present-day croft houses are
shown on Map 2 (p. 54).

CHAPTER ONE

Setting the Scene

Today the name Fair Isle is familiar to many, in the context of weather forecasts, complex and colourful knitting patterns, or exciting birdwatching. But not so long ago few had heard of this tiny island, which was until quite recently severed by remoteness and inaccessibility from the bustle and progress of the 'outside' world, while even fewer had set foot on it. Although its written historical record stretches back to Viking times, and there is archaeological evidence that it was inhabited from a much earlier date, Fair Isle was comparatively little visited by 'outsiders' — other than those unfortunate enough to be shipwrecked upon its rocky shores — until the 18th century. The accounts of those who did visit the isle, or who were involved in one way or another with the affairs of the folk who dwelt there, nevertheless provide a lively, albeit sometimes patchy, picture of the contemporary scene.

Life on the island has changed greatly since the earliest descriptions were recorded, and within the last 50 years has 'caught up with the Jones's' so that today's Fair Islanders enjoy most of the amenities that are taken for granted by mainland residents. The story of how these changes have come about, and the tenacity the folk have shown in clinging to their island home, at times in the face of deprivation and near despair, makes a fascinating background to the island as we see it today: a small but flourishing part of Scotland's natural and cultural heritage, held for the nation by the National Trust for Scotland and looking towards the 21st century with growing confidence.

Fair Isle has been aptly described as 'a lofty, precipitous rock, rising where two seas meet, the North Sea and the Atlantic Ocean . . . surrounded by what is termed a Roost, which consists of rough and troubled seas, arising from contrary currents conflicting, forming whirls and welchies, and frequently running at a rapid rate, in contrary directions, within a few hundred yards, which makes the Island difficult

1

Some of the most spectacular cliff scenery is along the north and west coasts, where steep slabs of bare rock alternate with less sheer vegetated slopes, and the shore is fringed with stacks and skerries. The area around the Stacks of Skroo (to the right) is a favourite haunt of grey seals, while in summer non-breeding gannets now whiten the 'roof' of Kirk Stack, the outer of the two.

of access . . .'. Early writers agreed on the approximate position of the island, 'near about the midst between Orkney and Zetland' (though some old maps place it much nearer the southern tip of Shetland), but not always on other matters relating to it. While some took 'Fayre' at face value, as meaning beautiful, others recorded the origin of the name variously as 'Faire Island so called because of the high white rocks which are seen afar off', and 'supposed to be a corruption of the Norse *Fjoer* or distant; or *Faar*, a sheep', while it has also been suggested that the name was originally 'Fire Island', perhaps from the beacons lit on its heights. The 'high white rocks' explanation seems unlikely to be valid, as little if any of Fair Isle's coastline could be described as white. 'Distant' and 'sheep' would both be appropriate — sheep have long been grazed on the island — while such epithets as 'beauty' are probably much influenced by the state of mind of the observer! The present consensus is, however, that Fair Isle derives from Fridarey, meaning truce isle, the name used for the island in the 'Orkneyinga Saga'.

'The coast of Fair Isle is the wildest and most unpitying that we have seen. Continuous cliffs, from one to four hundred feet high, tower by huge voes and echoing caverns, and line the bare downs with scarcely a curve of sand or a practicable cleft in the belt of iron precipices'. Robert Louis Stevenson and his father, lighthouse engineer Tom, clearly found that view from seaward awe-inspiring during their visit in 1869. A few years later it evoked a rather more lyrical description from another traveller: 'The island, rising out of the sea, looked a bright spot as we passed it; a solid rock of defence . . . The rains and the winds beat upon the towering rocks, and the mists rise up and conceal it ever and anon; but it bids all defiance, and stands there a fortress of the ages, firm and sure'. And one of the most famous of Fair Isle's visitors early this century, the Duchess of Bedford, noted in her diary: 'It is a very picturesque island, with steep crags and wonderful caves and arches . . . The view (in this case from the western cliffs, looking straight down into the sea from a height of more than 150 metres) is altogether beyond my description . . . Never in the whole of my travels have I seen any wild, rugged coast scenery which surpasses or even equals it'.

The spectacular stacks, arches and caves that are such a feature of the island's coastline are the result of continuous wear by weather and the sea, which nibble away at the medium-grained sandstones of which Fair Isle is largely composed. Erosion is fastest where faults cut across the bedding of the sandstones, leaving planes of shattered rock which is readily removed by wave action. As one nineteenth century writer put it, on Fair Isle 'the process of cave-making is made very plain, layer after layer being washed off by the upward action of the water, each layer as it peels off making the arch higher'. Eventually the roof falls in, sometimes along the whole length of the cave, so that a deep geo (miniature fjord) is created, and sometimes only in part. Both stages are represented at the Reevas on the west coast, where the final arch over the north Reeva fell in early this century. At the Kirn (churn) of Skroo, near the North Light, caves some 80 metres long link the sea to an inland blow-hole; with a northerly gale the sea roars in through these underground tunnels and churns fiercely around the hole in an awe-inspiring demonstration of

On days like this — when a north-easterly gale whips up the sea around Buness and sweeps a trail of spume in past the pier — the short-comings of the North Haven as a harbour become apparent; it offers 'no safe winter harbour'. Beyond the island's only sandy beach stands the original bird observatory, with the long finger of nearby Landberg promontory pointing left towards Sheep Craig. Other landscape features visible are the airstrip (not in use when this photo was taken in 1962), Malcolm's Head (top right) and the south lighthouse.

frustrated power. In time, no doubt, the roof here will also give way to the battering waves — for these cliffs are not really the 'iron precipices' that the Stevensons saw, but of much softer and more easily carved material.

The problems of landing on an island so extensively cliff-bound and so fringed with hazardous stacks and skerries impressed many of Fair Isle's early visitors. Buchanan, writing in the 16th century, described the isle as 'every way inaccessible save that towards the North East it, being a little lower, affords a harbour safe enough for small ships'. Perhaps Buchanan's visit — if indeed he made one — was in summer, since the shortcomings of the North Haven as a winter harbour were soon recognised by other writers. Surprisingly few references are made in these early descriptions to the South Harbour, which was for hundreds of years the focus of island-based sea-going — and the site of many a shipwreck. It must, however, have been quite widely known, as a French explorer who sailed along the south coast in the 1770s commented 'It seems to me that it is in this spot, at the foot of the hill, that the anchorage lies which is marked on the Dutch map, for the coast there forms a cove where one would be sheltered from the winds from the NW to NE'.

Not all the early descriptions of the size and shape of the island are readily recognisable, probably because some at least were second-hand. Most agree, however, that Fair Isle is a high-lying land, with several prominent hills or headlands, among them the 'strangely shaped hummock' of Sheep Craig. Rev. James Kay, Minister of Dunrossness Parish in the late 17th century, noted 'three hills or Promontories: two in the West Side: one near the south end called Malcolm's Head; another near the north end called the Wart, and a third on the east side called Vasseter, to which is adjoined the Sheep Craig, a very high rock about a quarter of a mile in circumference'. Kay reports that the only entry to Sheep Craig is from the sea, and goes on to describe the narrow neck of land linking the bottom of the Craig with the Vaasetter cliffs, concluding with the statement 'within these 40 or 50 years it was levell ground'. If this is true — and there is no way of checking — there must have been a most impressive rock fall as the 'bridge' gave way, perhaps during a particularly violent storm.

Kay's estimate of the island's size was a bit on the small side. He assessed it as 'in length from north to south, three miles; but very narrow, not exceeding a large half mile in the broadest place. The Hollanders . . . reckon it three leagues in circumference'. Measuring such an indented coastline is far from easy, but the overall length and maximum breadth of the isle are now known to be approximately 5½ kilometres (3¼ miles) and 2½ kilometres (1½ miles) respectively. Ward Hill rises to 217 metres above sea level, Malcolm's Head to 107 metres and Vaasetter to a little over 100 metres. From the highest point on Sheep Craig the cliff falls 132 metres sheer to the sea below, while the highest of the west side cliffs is about 180 metres.

Few of the earlier descriptions give much information about the general appearance of the island's interior, though one refers to a 'green table-land within' and Kay points out that 'there are no Forrests, Woods, nor Parks here . . . no Lochs, no Rivers, no Trees, no Broom, no Whins.' Then, as now, the greenest part was towards the south end, where all the present croft lands and houses are concentrated, but archaeological survey has shown that both habitations and cultivations were more widely scattered in an earlier period. The soil of the cultivated area is largely a reddish-brown sandy boulder clay deposited by the glaciers which passed over the island during the ice age. These same ice sheets were also responsible for moulding the NW—SE trending rocky ridges on which most of the present houses are built. To the north the croftland is bounded by the hill dyke, beyond which lies the common grazing or scattald, basically heather moorland interspersed with boggy hollows. When man first settled on Fair Isle much more of the island was probably covered with this type of wind-flattened and salt-blasted vegetation.

Because Fair Isle is such a prominent landmark amid the seas between Orkney and Shetland, the chances of rowing and sailing boats coming ashore there while making the crossing must always have been high. The earliest settlers in the Dunrossness district of Shetland are believed to have arrived more than 5,000 years ago, probably coming from further south in coracles or some similar fragile craft, and Man may well have first reached Fair Isle at about the same time. The archaeological evidence currently available indicates that the island has been inhabited for at least 3,000 years.

The presence of burnt mounds and other evidence of early occupation was first recorded more than 100 years ago, but recent field surveys by Bradford University have identified a remarkable wealth of prehistoric sites, many of which are in a surprisingly good state of preservation, largely because they lie outwith the area of relatively recent cultivation. In valley bottoms at Sukka Moor, Homisdale and Ferny Cup the signs of early settlement include traces of field boundaries, terraced earthworks, and enclosures suggestive of late neolithic/early Iron Age dwellings. More obvious to the untutored eye are the burnt mounds, heaps of blackened stones believed to have been used for cooking purposes; the mound situated slightly north of Pund and west of Vaasetter is one of the largest in Shetland. Urns made of pottery and soapstone, and what was thought to be cremation ash, were found in a mound near Finniquoy during road construction in the 1870s, and other possible burial sites have been located on Buness and near the cliff-edge at Mopul.

One of Fair Isle's most important monuments is the promontory fort at Landberg, a narrow, steep-sided headland near the North Haven. A defensive site protected by a series of stone-reinforced ramparts and ditches, the fort probably dates from the Iron Age but may have been reoccupied in Mediaeval times. Pottery sherds and a flint flake have been found there, and elsewhere on the island flint core axes and stone pounders have been picked up.

By the 10th century the Vikings were invading and battling over most parts of northern Scotland, and recording their deeds of daring in the sagas. Reference to Fair Isle appears in the 10th century 'Story of Burnt Njal': 'Those messmates Kari and Kolbein the Black put out from Eyrar (in Iceland) . . . got a fair wind and were but a short time out. The first land they made was the Fair Isle . . . There that man whose name was David the White took Kari into his house . . . and Kari stayed with him for the winter.'

The process of geo formation is well illustrated in this view; an arch still closes
the seaward end of the South Reeva, but the Round Reeva became a geo when
its arch fell in early this century. Signs of former cultivation stripe the fields
around the two Shirvas (Post Office to the left and Nurse's House to the right),
both enlarged some 30 years ago by adding wings. At top left the coastguard
lookout hut and ruined watchtower on Malcolm's Head are just visible.

The 'Orkneyinga Saga' tells of the role played by the isle in the 1130s during the struggle for supremacy between Earl Rognvald, who claimed part of Orkney, and Earl Paul, who was already established there. While celebrating after driving Rognvald back to Shetland, Earl Paul had the bright idea that he could obtain advance warning of any future retaliatory attack by establishing a chain of beacons 'to be lit if a host were seen coming from Shetland'. A beacon was duly piled up on Ward Hill and put under the charge of Dagfinn, 'who had an estate on Fair Isle'. However, the opposition were crafty too. A number of ships set sail from Shetland and came within sight of Fair Isle, then slowly raised their sails while oarsmen held the boats stationary. Dagfinn, thinking the boats were coming nearer, set fire to the beacon — whereupon they turned back to Shetland. Seeing the Fair Isle beacon alight, the look-outs on North Ronaldsay and further south all in turn lit theirs, so that 'Earl Paul's men mustered in huge numbers' — only to discover that it was a false alarm. In the ensuing argument Dagfinn was killed by the North Ronaldsay beacon-minder, and responsibility for Fair Isle's beacon passed to Eric.

Meantime four of Rognvald's men, led by Uni, had crossed to Fair Isle and set up house there, Uni pretending that he was a Norwegian who had been robbed by Earl Rognvald. Pleading that he had nothing else to do, Uni persuaded Eric to let him watch the beacon — and as soon as he was left alone he soaked it with water (which must have been quite a laborious task in view of the beacon's location!). Shortly after, with favourable wind and tide, Rognvald and his men set sail again. As the sodden Fair Isle beacon would not light no warning went ahead, and Rognvald reached and conquered Westray without trouble. Needless to say, Uni had made a rapid exit from the scene by the time Eric appeared.

Apart from a report of the death from exposure of the King of Norway's tax collector, who was wrecked on the isle in 1264 on his way to Orkney, there is no further written record of Viking activities on Fair Isle. Their long connection with the island is, however, evident from the maintenance for many centuries of the Viking tradition in boat design, and also from the fact that many of the words and place-names still in use today are of Old Norse origin. 'Grind' (gate) and 'moorit' (red — used of the red-brown sheep) are pure Norse, and the croft names of Setter (from saeter, an upland farm), Quoy (kvi, an enclosure for cattle) and Busta (a home or 'mother' settlement) are among the croft names of obviously Norse origin. The word 'scattald' has been used in relation to the common grazing since at least the late eighteenth century, but it derived originally from 'skat' (tax) and 'hald' (holding) and almost certainly referred to a piece of enclosed and cultivated ground.

All the crofts lie in the southern half of the island and all the houses other than
the Haa and Melville House (the two nearest the cemetery at lower right)
originally faced south-west, on much the same alignment as the rocky ridges
upon which most of them are sited. The small building in the right foreground
is the old lifeboat house — well inland from the beach!

Virtually no written records of Fair Isle exist for the 14th and 15th
centuries, but from the mid-16th century onwards the island is mentioned
increasingly often. Many of these early references relate to church affairs.
That the isle's first religious link was with the Catholic church in Orkney

is suggested by the fact that 'the duties of St Peter's Stouk' on Fair Isle — believed to refer to the stipend due on a small area of land belonging to the church — were in the 16th century paid to St Magnus Cathedral in Kirkwall. After the Reformation the stipend due on this stouk, 'ane barrell butter and ane noble or crown (30 shillings Scots)' was paid to the grammar school in Kirkwall as part of its endowment. Protestant teaching had apparently reached, but not entirely converted, the islanders by 1588, when a survivor of the Armada ship wrecked on the isle, doubtless himself a devout Catholic, wrote 'They are neither Christians nor altogether heretics. It is true that they confess that the doctrine that once a year is preached to them by people sent from an island 9 leagues off is not good; but they dare not contradict it'.

Proof that by then the island's religious links were with Shetland comes from an account of the assignation of stipends in 1576, in which Fair Isle is listed among the churches contributing to 'the haill vicarage of Dunrosnes', and — apart from a period of about 60 years during the 18th century when, incredibly, 'Fair Isle, Foully and Skery' were united to form 'the most discontiguous parish in Britain' — the island has ever since been part of Dunrossness Parish. A small place of worship apparently existed on the isle from the 17th century, perhaps considerably earlier; there is archaeological evidence to suggest an early Christian site close to the present cemetery above Kirkigeo, while tradition has it that there was once a kirk near Shirva, at a spot which still bears the name Kirkalees.

Although not exactly regular in their visitations, the ministers responsible for the welfare of Fair Isle souls did their best under difficult circumstances, and by the early 19th century the isle had its own resident 'catechist'. Many of these men left valuable accounts of the state of their flock. In addition to such obvious sources as the Statistical Accounts, information about the isle in the 18th and 19th centuries can be gleaned from a miscellaneous collection of writings — by passing explorers, casual visitors and lighthouse engineers, for example. The present century has seen the first systematic accounts of the island's wildlife, scientific and archaeological interest.

The many changes of ownership that Fair Isle has undergone in the last 400 years are rather unevenly documented, especially in the early days. What is probably the earliest specific reference dates from 1572, the year in which Earl Patrick succeeded his father Robert Stewart, illegitimate son of James V, to whom 'the lands of Orkney and Zeitland with the isles belonging thereto' had been granted by Royal Charter in 1564. A Feu Charter dated 1572, recording a transaction between Adam Bothwell, Bishop of Orkney and Zetland, and Robert Stewart concerning bishopric

Landberg promontory fort was a defensive site protected by a series of parallel ditches and earth ramparts. This view is looking northwards over the outer ramparts; the stone blocks in the foreground and at left flank the entrance gap. At top right is the Stack o' North Haven, which the proposed breakwater will link with Buness, giving protection to the pier and slipway even in a northerly gale.

lands, includes mention of 'nine merks (about 1/10 of the total arable area) of land lying in the isle of Fair Isle'. The Stewart Earls of Shetland probably held most of Fair Isle until about 1614, when Earl Patrick died, but they let it 'in feu' to others, usually non-resident 'proprietors' who in turn sub-let to resident 'tacksmen'. One of these proprietors was evidently 'J. Menteith of ye Fair Ill', recorded in the 1592 Register of the Privy Council of Scotland as among the signatories to a disclaimer by Orkney and Shetland lairds of any hostility to 'Patrick, Master of Orkney'. By 1624 69 merks of land on the isle were held under charter by James Sinclair of Quendale in Shetland, and two years later he apparently became proprietor of the whole island. His family remained lairds for three generations, until in 1766 Fair Isle was put on the market after the then owner, Robert Sinclair, had been declared bankrupt.

At the sale in Edinburgh the island was bought for £860 by James Stewart, a wealthy ship-owner of Brough, in Westray, Orkney. Shortly after he had purchased it, Stewart visited the isle with a farmer friend, Patrick Fea, who noted in his diary: 'Brough convened all the people of the isle, from whom he had little satisfaction, all pleading poverty so that he will recover little of their arrears.' When Stewart died in 1802 his estate passed to a nephew, also James Stewart, who was only 14 years old, and trustees were appointed to administer it until he came of age. The trustees commissioned Patrick Fotheringhame, a lawyer and Town Clerk of Kirkwall, to report on conditions in the island; his account is one of the fullest and most informative for that period. A third generation James Stewart was subsequently proprietor of the isle from infancy until he died, unmarried, in 1858, leaving the Brough Estates in the care of Trustees, largely for the benefit of the North Isles Presbytery in Orkney.

Before long the Trustees clearly came to the conclusion that Fair Isle was more a liability than an asset; the people were virtually destitute as a result of repeated crop failures and an ever-expanding population, and the Trustees were apparently reluctant to accept responsibility for trying to resolve the problem. In 1866 they put up for sale 'the 96 merks of land in Fair Isle, comprehending Leogh, Gila, Busta and Shirva with their pertinants'; the upset price was £2,500 and, after keen competition, the isle was sold to John Bruce of Sumburgh, Shetland, for £3,360, considered to be a very high price.

Bruce was fully aware of what he was taking on, as he had played a major part in making arrangements for a mass emigration of Fair Islanders four years earlier. Although he appears to have been concerned for the islanders' welfare and to have treated them reasonably fairly, his son, John Bruce the Younger, who leased the estate from him in 1872, was a harder business man, as is evident from his statements to the Truck and Crofters' Commission enquiries around the turn of the century. Nevertheless Fair Isle saw a good many improvements under the two Johns, and by the time John the Younger died in 1907 living conditions there were vastly better than they had been in 1866. Not all the improvements were initiated by Bruce, however; two other individuals also played important roles in island affairs towards the end of the 19th century. The first was teacher William Laurence, whose very practical approach to his responsibilities resulted in, among other things, the introduction of life-saving equipment and a postal service. In his endeavours on behalf of the islanders, Laurence was ably supported by George Thoms, Sheriff of Orkney and Zetland, whose contacts in Edinburgh and elsewhere enabled him to apply pressure on the authorities over such matters as the establishment of a money order office.

Two further Bruces, Robert Hunter, younger brother of John, and his nephew Robert Hunter Wingate (who took the surname Bruce) succeeded

Early morning light and lifting mist add a touch of drama to this view of the ancient burnt mound near Vaasetter croft; beyond, the summit of Sheep Craig rises above the mist. The mound is formed of stones which had been heated in a fire and then used to boil water for cooking purposes.

as lairds of Fair Isle, latterly under the umbrella of the Sumburgh Estate Co. Ltd. During 1947 the company decided to sell Fair Isle and early in 1948 George Waterston, who had visited the isle before the war and was already actively involved in trying to establish a bird observatory there, succeeded in acquiring it for £3,500, almost exactly the price paid by John Bruce in 1866. Fair Isle Bird Observatory opened in autumn 1948, bringing new hope for the island's future, but George Waterston soon realised that no private individual could undertake the many and varied improvements by then needed. Only six years after he had bought it he offered Fair Isle to the National Trust for Scotland, on the sole condition that money be found to repay the loan which had enabled him to purchase the island. The Dulverton Trust provided the necessary financial assistance, and since 1954 Fair Isle has been held inalienably by the National Trust for Scotland, who care for the island on the nation's behalf.

Estate papers and other documents from the Sinclair, Stewart and Bruce periods provide a fairly good picture of life in those days, while the story since 1948 has been fully documented. The wide range of written material relating to Fair Isle, when drawn together, builds up a picture of changing dependence upon sea and land, of long-lasting poverty and privation eventually giving way to prosperity, and of progressively decreasing isolation from the outside world. A major theme throughout this story has been the Fair Islanders' love of their rock-girt home.

CHAPTER TWO

Sea Area Fair Isle

Nobody who listens to the shipping forecast can be unaware of the fact that Fair Isle is frequently battered by gale force winds. These, together with its distance from the nearest land, the strong tides that churn the intervening seas, and the inhospitable nature of its coasts mean that for much of its inhabited history Fair Isle has had only tenuous and irregular contact with the outside world. 'Situated some 26 miles from North Ronaldsay, and 24 from Sumburgh Head in the full swirl of the Gulf Stream as it forces its way between the Orkneys and Shetlands, Fair Isle is a conspicuous example of matter in the wrong place' wrote J. R. Tudor in his 1883 book on Orkney and Shetland. 'Prominent enough in fair weather, it becomes during fogs, in snowstorms or during dark winter nights, owing to the strong sets of tide which sweep down on all sides of it, one of the most dangerous spots in the North Sea.' Tudor was pretty accurate with his distances (the isle is about 27 miles or 43 km ENE of North Ronaldsay and 24 miles or 39 km SW of Sumburgh Head) and he certainly summed up the main problems associated with Fair Isle's location very aptly.

Isolation, unpredictable weather and irregular communications affect many aspects of island life: the availability of medical help, food costs, and the risk of loss at sea, to name but a few. Over the centuries, and particularly during the last 50 years, much has been done to reduce Fair Isle's remoteness, in everything except the geographical sense. Today the island is in far closer touch with the outside world than in the past, but the progress in communications that brought this about has not been achieved without struggle. And one thing that has not changed is the weather which, according to the 1921 edition of the North Sea Pilot, is in winter notoriously 'stormy and thick in this region'.

On average Fair Isle endures 64 days every year in which the wind force exceeds 34 knots, while gusts of hurricane force (at least 64 knots) are not uncommon between October and March. 1979 was a notably windy year, with gale-force gusts recorded on 112 days, whereas the corresponding figure for 1985 was only 16. Gales drive huge waves hurtling against the cliffs, where they break with such force that great gobs of salty spume soar with the up-draught and are often wafted right across the island. High seas frequently throw large stones far inland; in low-lying areas such as Buness recently-moved rocks and the scars left by their travel are sometimes clearly visible. January is the worst month for gales but storms can occur in any of the winter months, and occasionally in summer too, often disrupting not only communications but also most other aspects of island life. In October 1948 'haystacks were blown all over the place' and a large hut on Ward Hill virtually disappeared; in 1961 an elderly islander's leg was broken when she was blown over and she could not be evacuated to hospital as travel by boat was impossible; in February 1967 the school closed early when warning of a storm force 10 gale was received, every child being accompanied home by an adult; and in March 1969 'a gale from the south-east drove sheets of salt water across the isle and destroyed what grass there was'.

Gales apart, the Fair Isle climate is much what one might expect for a small, but relatively high, island. Fog is most frequent in the period May-September. Ground frost and hail occur fairly often but air frost and lying snow are uncommon, and thunder is seldom recorded more than two or three times in a year. Records kept by the island's meteorologist for 1974-87 show that monthly mean temperatures ranged from 3.9°C in January to 11.8°C in August, the maximum only occasionally rising above 15°C even in mid-summer. Rainfall is in the region of 900mm a year, with November-December usually the wettest and May-June the driest, and the sunniest, months. Water is seldom in really short supply, although back in May 1881 grain had to be taken to Kirkwall for grinding, as there was insufficient water to drive the Fair Isle mills.

The islanders' descriptions for some weather conditions are picturesque, though they can be somewhat misleading! When Dodie Stout skippered the *Good Shepherd II* he used to refer to summer mist as 'lumps o' heat' and dismissed the heaving water of the Roost after a gale as a 'southerly tumble'. In 'Words, Phrases and Recollections from Fair Isle' Jerry Eunson records that sunbeams dancing are known as 'summer cloks'. And a good day between bad spells is 'a day atween weathers'.

Contrary tides, strong winds and frequent fog make Fair Isle waters hazardous for shipping and the island has long been equipped to provide warning to navigators and rescue for the shipwrecked. The first 'signal station' was not for the benefit of sailors, however. During the Napoleonic wars early in the 19th century a watchtower was erected on Malcolm's

Head, and from there observers kept a lookout for potential enemy ships. Contact was made with passing vessels by signalling with flags. According to Sir Walter Scott, who visited the isle in 1814, 'When any ship appears that cannot answer his signal, he (James Strong, in charge of the station) sends off to Lerwick and Kirkwall to give the alarm', presumably by despatching an island yole; as Scott was departing 'the signal-post displayed its flags'. Beacons were still also employed as signals at least occasionally until well through the 19th century. In 1877, for example, 'a signal fire made it known that something unusual (a wreck) had occurred' and the writer bemoaned the 'want of lighthouses and a lifeboat', a need which the island's teacher, William Laurence, a former officer in the Mercantile Marine, had already pointed out to government, going straight to the top by writing direct to Disraeli. That same year Captain Prowse, HM Inspector of Lifesaving Apparatus, visited the isle 'to determine the question of the establishment of a life-saving apparatus, lifeboat or lighthouse on the island'. Since then warning signals have become progressively more sophisticated, eventually reaching the computer-age in the 1980s.

Fair Isle's first lifeboat, which was also the first in Shetland, was delivered in 1878 by the Board of Trade, who paid nearly every man on the isle a 10/— retainer for manning it. A replacement arrived in 1911, when the seamanship of the men who went out in a NW gale to collect it from the steamer was much admired by the Duchess of Bedford. The third, and last, lifeboat, designed for the job and equipped with a 12/14 hp petrol/paraffin engine, was paid for (as were many other 'improvements') with money received for wreck salvage. At the time of its delivery in 1924 the urgent need for a convenient slipway was noted, but 21 years later a visitor commented that 'There is a sort of motor life-boat here kept in a shed far (about 80 metres!) from the sea, but no means of launching are available'. The lifeboat service was withdrawn soon after — fortunately, rescue work is not dependent upon the availability of an island lifeboat.

The lifesaving apparatus brought to the isle along with the first lifeboat doubtless included equipment similar to the rocket lines and breeches buoys in use by the coastguard service until early in 1988. Responsibility for cliff rescue work still lies with the coastguards, but helicopters have now taken over for all 'lift-off' rescues from wrecks — depriving the more adventurous onlooker of a chance to sample a 'dry' ride in the breeches buoy during the regular training sessions. The coastguards are also responsible for the 'bad weather watch', which is mounted at times of severe gales. From the lookout shelter near the ruins of the old signal station on the summit of Malcolm's Head the duty coastguard scans the

17

Rough seas, steep cliffs and deep water often combine to make it impossible to prevent the loss of a vessel even when those on board can be brought to safety; such was the case with this fishing boat, the *Norseman's Bride*. Wrecks are a mixed blessing for the islanders, however; though rescues may be risky the resultant flotsam often proves useful.

horizon for shipping in distress — and occasionally takes advantage of his elevated viewpoint to observe what his relatives and friends are up to, as I learned when called into the Post Office to take a phone call from the look-out! With the advent of radar the risk of ships being wrecked on the isle in fog is now minimal, and fog watches are no longer operated.

Although the desirability of establishing a lighthouse on Fair Isle had been noted as early as 1809 little happened until 1867, when the first definite proposal was turned down — partly on the grounds that there had been 'only one wreck within our recollection' — and a fog signal was suggested as an alternative. Ten years passed without progress, but by 1877 the Northern Lighthouse Board was receiving petitions regarding lights on Fair Isle from many different shipping interests, local-based and from as far afield as Germany. D. & T. Stevenson, Engineers to the Board, were asked to submit a report and a visit was made in July 1877, when the party was met at the South Harbour by William Laurence. The following year it was recommended that a light and a fog-signal be placed on each end of the island. As money was tight at the time the Stevensons suggested, however, that if funds would only rise to one light it might be best placed on Malcolm's Head 'and could be constructed in such a manner as to admit of easy removal to the lower site when the complete system of lighting comes to be carried out'.

That suggestion was not implemented and work on the lighthouses did not begin for another 12 years, but in 1885 the first fog-warning system on the island, an experimental rocket station, was established. Designed to explode at about 800 feet above sea level, so as to avoid the sound shadows created by the heights of Sheep Craig and Ward Hill, the rockets were fired at 10 minute intervals 'in thick weather and snow showers'. The ruins of the rocket station, which operated for only a year, and its associated explosives store can still be seen near the hill dyke.

In 1890 construction of the two lighthouses started at long last. A team of 34 workmen, including an inspector of public works, four quarrymen, eight masons and a blacksmith, was involved; 12 of them lived in a one-window bothy and two were accommodated in the shelter built at 'Terrafield' for the rocket-firers. The South Light, atop a tower 26 metres high, was lit for the first time in January 1892 and the North Light, standing a mere 14 metres above the 75 metre high Skroo cliffs, in November that year. An innovative lamp design, called by its developers, the Stevensons, a 'hyper-radiant apparatus', was introduced for the North Light; an increased focal distance between the centre of the light source (a paraffin lamp) and the inside of the glass cage permitted a greater intensity of light to be produced without the whole system overheating. Superseded equipment from the Isle of May was used in the South Light.

In theory the powerful lighthouse foghorns can be heard 40 km away, but curious acoustical quirks result in occasional 'deaf spots'. I remember

Fair Isle's first lifeboat arrived in 1878; the one pictured here is probably its successor, which operated from 1911 until 1924. The Duchess of Bedford was much impressed by the seamanship of its crew, but it is hard to believe that either the lifejackets of the day or the inconveniently located lifeboat shed were of much benefit to the service.

one foggy trip in the 1950s when the north horn could not be heard from the *Good Shepherd* until she was less than 1½ km from the island, and there was an unfortunate incident in 1901 when the mail steamer *St Rognvald*, with a Northern Lighthouse Board Superintendent on board, struck the north end of the isle in fog. Although the Superintendent never heard the horn himself 'inquiry showed that it had been sounding continuously'; automatic recorders were fitted soon after and a modern 'screech' has now replaced the horn.

For 86 years manning of the two lighthouses meant the addition of six light-keepers and their families to the island population, and provided part-time employment for several islanders, not only at the lights themselves but also during the regular visits of the lighthouse supply boat *Pole Star*. The first change in this situation came in 1978, when the North Light was made a 'rock station' with the keepers' families living in Stromness and the men being flown in each month by helicopter. But as far back as 1945 George Waterston had predicted that 'with the strides being made in modern science, the day may come when the lighthouses on Fair Isle will be operated by "remote control"'. That day eventually came in 1982, when the North Light was automated, involving removal of the original lighting apparatus, with its weight-driven gearing, and replacement with an electrically driven revolving system and battery operated lamps. A computer known as 'Fiona' took over responsibility for alerting the keepers still resident at the South Light, now classed as a rock station, when a fault occurs. No doubt that light too will be automated in due course.

Even with the advent of lighthouses and foghorns the toll of vessels coming to grief on Fair Isle's dangerous coastline did not end, although the numbers lost decreased greatly. In the days of sail (which lasted into the early years of this century) the wind drove many ships ashore; more recently fog and navigational errors have been the commonest causes of disaster; and a surprising number of boats have been lost or damaged while seeking shelter, or at anchor, in the South Harbour and North Haven. Over the years the Fair Islanders have saved the lives of many seafarers, often at considerable risk to themselves. Occasionally they have been rewarded with money; more often they have simply benefited from the goods and timber salvaged after a ship had broken up completely.

Little is known about the wrecks that occurred prior to the 19th century, with one notable exception: El Gran Grifon, a support ship of the Spanish Armada which, being in dire straits from storm damage and shortage of water, was deliberately driven ashore at Stroms Heelor, near the south-east corner of the island, in late September 1588. The story of her adventures both before and after the wreck is well documented; one of those on board kept a diary and there are contemporary accounts of the survivors' arrival in Anstruther en route for home. By a merciful providence the Grifon stuck fast on the rocks with her mast leaning against the cliff and the 300 or so men aboard all managed to scramble ashore. This sudden increase in the population of an ill-provided island posed real problems of survival. For seven long weeks the islanders did what they could for their uninvited guests but some 50 Spaniards died of starvation; the food situation had become desperate by the time the remainder were taken off to Shetland after a yole had crossed to Grutness seeking relief. Salvage operations at the wreck were proposed in 1593 and actually attempted in 1740, when two brass guns were raised. More systematic searching by a team of maritime archaeologist divers during the 1970s resulted in recovery of a variety of guns, shot and other items. When 35 Spaniards, attired in 16th century military costume, complete with standards, weapons and other accoutrements, visited Fair Isle in July 1984, to commemorate the loss of El Gran Grifon and record thanks for the island's part in saving her crew, international relations were much happier than they had been some 400 years earlier.

There seems to be no record of 17th century wrecks, of which there were doubtless many, while those in the 18th century included some

21

with cargoes of timber — always useful on a treeless island — and a few Dutch fishing boats sunk near the isle by French privateers. In the 1800s the islanders' gallantry in saving life earned them rewards on several occasions. By far the largest-scale rescue was mounted in 1868 when, in gale and mist, the *Lessing* became wedged in the mouth of Claver Geo, on the south coast of Vaasetter. On board were 465 German emigrants heading for New York. Unable to come alongside the stricken vessel because of heavy seas, the islanders manoeuvred their yoles through an arch leading to Claver Geo inshore of the wreck. All the passengers and crew were taken back through the arch and up the cliff with the help of ropes. The German government's reward of £100 for this daring rescue was distributed among the men and boys who had assisted, much to the indignation of the island women, who felt that they too deserved some recompense for housing and feeding the survivors for 10 days.

Several fishing boats have been lost this century, among them the *Strathbeg*, which was unpopular with the Fair Islanders as she frequently trawled within traditional island fishing grounds. When she struck in dense fog her crew took to their lifeboat and rowed to seaward, fearing ill-treatment at the hands of the islanders! Later, however, they were brought ashore in the island lifeboat — and soon discovered that their fears were unfounded. More recently the island mailboat has been involved in two rescues. During stormy weather in January 1975 three crewmen were plucked to safety in a yole launched from the deck of the *Good Shepherd III* after the Kirkwall-registered *Norseman's Bride* had run ashore near the North Light. And in September 1980 the mailboat joined other vessels in an unsuccessful attempt to haul the *Maverick* off the 'shark's teeth' known as Da Rivvicks, outside the South Harbour. This last wreck happened on a fine summer night. The *Maverick*, an almost new Shetland trawler, had completed the hauling-in of a big catch off Meoness and her crew, busy gutting fish under the deck shelter, failed to notice that the ebb tide was carrying the boat rapidly westward — until her bottom bumped on the rocks. Even close familiarity with the hazards of the island's coastline is no guarantee of safety; Fair Isle's first two island-based mailboats were both driven ashore in the North Haven.

The Haven's shortcomings as an anchorage were noted by Rev. James Kay during his pastoral visitations; in his view 'Here small ships may ride safe enough in ye summer time, but it is no good winter harbour.' The problems posed by difficult landings and poor harbourage long hindered efforts to establish, and later improve, regular sea links between Fair Isle and the outside world. In Kay's day, and for the following 200 years, contact with Shetland, and Orkney, was both sporadic and chancy. In 1753 Rev. John Mill hitched a lift on a Dutch fishing vessel, but when he was dropped off in his small boat near the isle 'The wind and tide was contrary, the night coming on and a mist forming . . . I was seized with a great fear'. In 1799 another visiting minister set off from Shetland in a six-oared boat which unfortunately missed Fair Isle and the following morning 'landed at Sanda in the Orkneys by a favourable providence, when the wind shifted suddenly to the south for return of the boat next day'. More than 24 hours in a small open boat is not an experience many people would relish, even in those days.

The more-or-less annual visit by the minister continued to be the only regular communication with the rest of Shetland until the late 19th century, although there would, of course, be occasional trips to Grutness or Orkney by island boats and visits to the isle by bigger vessels in connection with the fishing trade. A suggestion that the Kirkwall-Lerwick packet boat should call occasionally for mails was put forward in 1863, when an article in Chambers Journal commented that 'A letter to India or Australia might arrive as soon as one from Fair Isle to London'. Eventually, in 1877, a fortnightly 'regular' mail service started, with the islanders going off in a yole to rendezvous with the northern isles steamer. Although a packet-boat from Sumburgh also carried passengers as well as goods, this was the means whereby most people reached or left the island, as it would continue to be until well into this century.

But this arrangement was less than satisfactory. As the Duchess of Bedford commented in 1909 'If the weather does not permit, it (the post) apparently waits another fortnight as the mail steamer simply passes by on the other side'. And a visitor in 1931 wrote 'It is not easy to effect a landing; there is always the risk of a mishap, and the regular steamers discourage the process. They certainly make passengers pay for the privilege'. The cost when travel writer H. V. Morton came to Fair Isle in 1935 was 27/− to be put off the steamer plus the full fare to Shetland. Just how difficult the landing could be is illustrated by the experiences of teacher Alexander Doloughan who arrived with his family in November 1933, coming ashore from the *St Rognvald* in a north-east gale; the party not only had to cope with the transfer from ship to 'sixern' but also had to scramble up the cliffs of the geo in which they landed. When the family left the isle in December 1937 they opted to go by air! (This was a one-off opportunity which pre-dated Fair Isle's scheduled air service by nearly 40 years.)

Meanwhile, in 1921, a more reliable and regular sea-link had been established, this time operating from Fair Isle itself. The previous year six islanders had clubbed together to buy an ex-lifeboat, with the intention of using her for fishing. Their hopes in this respect proved over-optimistic, however, and their financial prospects looked poor until the Post Office

In 1982 the North Light's paraffin lamp was lit for the last time, to be replaced on automation with a battery-powered beam. It was here that, just 90 years earlier, the Stevensons introduced their innovative 'hyper-radiant apparatus'.

When the first car, a baby Austin, arrived aboard *Good Shepherd I* in 1936 unloading was clearly a tricky business, even though it was high tide and flat calm. Until the late 1950s neither the island's mailboat nor its pier was capable of handling all types of freight at all states of the tide.

offered them a contract; the *Good Shepherd* carried her first mails on 21 May 1921. Although rather under-powered for the Roost — she regularly took 5-6 hours to cross to Grutness and was often unable to return the same day — the original *Good Shepherd* served the isle well until on 3 January 1937, while at anchor in the North Haven (with a bow rope attached to the stack described 250 years earlier as 'good for fixing a land-rope'), she was driven ashore by a gale and became a total loss.

Good Shepherd II, a slightly larger wooden fishing boat, started her long and eventful career in May 1937, under the same ownership and with the same crew as her predecessor. To ensure that she did not suffer a similar fate the inadequate slipway built on the North Haven beach in 1923 underwent major improvements, and throughout the winter she was hauled up between her weekly trips. But in January 1947, while the slipway and man-powered winch were temporarily out of action and the service was being operated from Lerwick by a crew of only three, *GSII* also came ashore in the Haven, though what could easily have been a disaster was mercifully averted. Snatching at the chance of 'a day atween weathers' the crew had left Lerwick six hours earlier with a home-coming stretcher patient battened down in the hold. By the time they reached Fair Isle an easterly gale had blown up but they managed to fight their way through the seas breaking across the mouth of the Haven, and caught up the mooring buoy — only for it to give way under the strain. With an anchor dropped and the engine kept running all might yet have gone well, but a vital bolt suddenly broke, the engine stopped and within seconds *GSII* was aground. Fortunately she was lying with her deck facing the beach, making it possible for all the passengers and goods to be carried safely ashore. The boat was out of service for more than a year — and immediate steps were taken by the then Zetland County Council to plan for a better slipway with power-driven winch. These improvements came none too soon; by the time they were completed in 1954 there were barely enough able-bodied men left on the island to operate the old hand-driven winch.

In the early years of her service *GSII*, like her predecessor, was able to come alongside the original lighthouse pier in the North Haven only at very high tide; at all other times goods and passengers had to be ferried ashore in a 'flit boat', a process which involved multiple handling of goods and an awkward scramble for passengers. Proposals and planning for a deep-water extension started in 1955 and the present pier was in use by the end of 1958. In the meantime the county council had agreed to take over responsibility for the Fair Isle ferry service and to start twice-weekly sailings during the summer. The *GSII* was also undergoing major improvements: a more powerful engine installed in 1955 reduced the

Having to bring both goods and passengers ashore by 'flit-boat', because the *Good Shepherd II* could only come alongside at high tide, prolonged loading and unloading and also involved double manhandling of a large proportion of the freight. This situation changed when the pier was extended in 1958.

crossing time slightly, while the new deck-house fitted in 1968 provided passengers with much-needed protection from the elements. Just as valuable was the radio, financed by a collection taken among passengers on an early National Trust for Scotland cruise. Now the crew could maintain contact with the isle during the crossing, enabling the reception party of cars and lorries to time its arrival at the pier with much greater accuracy and meals to be got ready at exactly the right time.

Good Shepherd III, a second-hand steel trawler for which Zetland County Council, the Scottish Office and the crew together paid £27,000, took over the service in 1972. Although much more powerful, so that crossing times were less influenced by the weather, and an excellent sea-boat, she was not ideal for either cargo-handling or passengers. Portholes high above eye-level and a combination of high-riding and heavy ballasting made her peculiarly uncomfortable for all but those with the least responsive of stomachs! There were few regrets when she was 'retired' to the Papa Stour service in 1986. It was during the *GSIII* era, in 1981, that an entirely new slip, leading into a 'noost' quarried out of Buness, was constructed on the outer side of the pier. This location is more sheltered than the old slip and can be used safely under a greater range of wind directions — one more step in improving the North Haven's qualities as a winter harbour.

Unlike any of her predecessors, *Good Shepherd IV* was designed for her particular task, and equipped to do it as efficiently as possible. Her 360hp diesel engine has reduced the crossing time from Grutness to 2½ hours. Her generators power lighting throughout — and TV, cooker and fridge in the galley. With a carrying capacity of more than 30 tons, and a crane capable of a two-ton lift, she can handle all island imports and exports, including cars, coal and container-loaded livestock. Radar, radio and radio-telephone ensure that she can maintain contact with both her destination and other shipping — and greatly reduce the risk of collision, with either the isle or another vessel, during fog. And her passenger accommodation is much improved, with toilet facilities and reclining seats. My only critical comment after my first trip on her was that seat belts might be a good idea — the Roost still produces what Dodie would have called 'a bit of motion'!

Two other important, though less obvious, developments coincided with the arrival of the *GSIV*. All financial responsibility for the ferry service passed to Shetland Islands Council, who received European Economic Community grant for the boat's purchase and employ the four-man crew on a part-time basis; paid on an hourly rate the crew no longer suffer financially if bad weather causes delays in returning to the isle. And an extra service was introduced, with fortnightly trips right to Lerwick throughout the summer; this is of great value in reducing freight costs on incoming goods, especially bulky or heavy items such as furniture and coal.

More than 100 years have passed since teacher William Laurence sought financial assistance from the Treasury to improve harbour facilities on Fair Isle. His proposal involved the South Harbour where, he thought, a breakwater 'could be very easily and inexpensively formed by joining several rocks to one another and to the shore'; that project was not, however, considered practicable. In the last 50 years much has been done to improve facilities at the North Haven but, despite the new pier and slipway and the bigger and better boat, bad weather can still make it unsafe to operate there and the island's sea link with Shetland remains at the mercy of the weather. Only one development could change this situation — the construction of a breakwater linking Buness and the Stack of the North Haven, a proposal first put forward by George Waterston in 1945. Serious consideration was not given to this suggestion until 1978, since when costs have rocketed and no firm commitment has yet been made. But with such a development recommended in the Council of Europe's Diploma Award of 1985, and the prospect of Regional Development Fund money becoming available, hopefully before too much longer the comment 'no good winter harbour' will cease to be true of Fair Isle. As well as making the *Good Shepherd* service more reliable, the existence of a safe harbour might also make it practicable to revive the fishing industry, which was of such value to the island in the past.

Only the construction of a breakwater to protect the slipway and pier would make it safe to launch *Good Shepherd IV* in conditions like these. At present when northerly gales sweep into the Haven she must remain in the 'noost', or dry berth, cut out of Buness for her.

CHAPTER THREE

Harvesting the Seas

The turbulent seas round Fair Isle support numerous fish of many different kinds. According to James Robertson, who visited the isle in 1769, 'The coast is stored with the same kinds of fish that are found on the coast of Shetland, such as Cod, Ling, Tusk, Seth, Skate, Holybut, Dogfish, etc., besides a great variety of Shelfish'. At that time the islanders were almost totally dependent upon fishing for their livelihood — a situation which existed from the 16th century, and probably earlier, to the end of the 19th century, although fish populations, fishing techniques and marketing arrangements all changed over this period. Since the early 1900s fishing has steadily declined in importance and it is now of no economic significance to the islanders.

One of the earliest descriptions of the Fair Isle fishery comes from Rev. James Kay: '. . . the chiefest income of this Isle is Fishes, whereof they have great plenty . . . . . . Seath, Sea dogs (here called Hoes) and Podlocks (here Piltocks) are very beneficial by reason of the Oyl which they make of their livers. Of the Fishes which they take (such as are for their own use) some they eat fresh, some they hang in Skeos till they are sour and these they call blown fishes. Such as they design for Merchant-ware, some they salt, some they hang fresh in Skeos until they be perfectly dry and these they call Stock fishes, whereof they have great plenty here'.

No traces now remain of the skeos (small dry-stone sheds) but an old map shows two groups situated along the Brecks o' Leogh and on Meoness, both sites where the prevailing south-westerly winds would sweep up-slope from the sea, ensuring a good through-flow of drying air. These sites were conveniently close to the noosts at Leestat and at Kirkigeo (South Harbour), where the boats were based and near which there was 'a Booth built by Quendale, Proprietor of the Isle, for the use of a Hamburgh Merchant, who used to ly there and make Merchant Fishes'. The exact site of that booth is not known but there was certainly a store

When the Fair Isle fishery was in its heyday large quantities of fish were dried on the man-made pebble beach near Kirkigeo. The building in the background is the old fish store, now extended to form the Puffinn where voluntary work parties are based.

and warehouse in use near the South Harbour for more than 200 years. The final stone-built structure now forms the 'heart' of the Puffinn where voluntary work parties visiting the island are accommodated.

The 'Hamburgh Merchant' was one of many 'foreign adventurers' involved in the Shetland fish trade during the 17th century. These merchants arrived in the spring, bringing with them grain, which they sold to the islanders, and 'all the apportions and implements necessary for their prosecuting the Fisheries'. Throughout the summer they salted, cured and dried the fish they bought as the boats came in, and at the end of the season they exported not only the fish but also any other goods, such as oil, skins and hosiery, that they were able to buy locally. Although trade with visitors was discouraged on the isle, the landlord had no control over what happened at sea, and much bartering was done off-shore. In addition to paying the fishermen, the merchants had to pay an agreed sum (often 1d per large fish — mainly cod, the closely-related ling, and tusk or torske) to the proprietor 'for the privilege granted these traders of erecting their booths and warehouses and of carrying on their traffic on the landlord's ground'.

A progressive increase in the levies demanded of the foreign merchants, together with the introduction of a tax on foreign salt, eventually brought an end to the activities of Fair Isle's 'Hamburgh Merchant' and for a time the trading in fish was carried on by merchants based in Dundee. A document dated 1695 records that 'Laurence Sinclair of Quendale sets the Fayre yland in tack (lease) to Robert Kerr, factor for James Alisone, John Smith, Thomas Cowan and George and Robert Watsones, all Merchants in Dundee, and all the whole fishings of the boates pertaining to his tennants . . . . on the following conditions: For each hundredth ling gildit, £18 Scots. Ilk gullion of Stockfish the sum of 32/— per gullion. Ilk leispend of Butter the sum of 56/— Scots. Ilk barrell of Oylie £18 Scots. And Laurence Sinclair to fraught his great boat to the said Robert Kerr for transporting such fisch butter and oylie from the said Fair yland to Dunrossnes and to saill when requyred wind and weather serving.' The terms 'gullion' and 'leispend' (or lispund) refer to parts of Shetland's very complex system of measures and weights, which were used as standards for barter. As they did not remain constant it is not easy to guess at modern equivalents — but the names themselves have a certain fascination.

There is no record of how long the Dundee merchants traded on Fair Isle, but early in the 18th century the Shetland lairds took all such matters into their own hands, operating what became known as the Truck (meaning barter or exchange) System and has also been described as 'debt-bondage'. As James Robertson put it 'the . . . fishery is carried on at the expense of the Landed Gentlemen, the Vassals of each being bound to fish for his Superior and for him only. To him every fish must be offered in the first instance, and the price, which generally amounts to three pence the fish, is fixed by the Gentlemen themselves. They supply the Fishermen with Boats, Lines, Provisions, etc. for which they are paid in fish. When any Fisherman is dismissed by a Gentleman for the atrocious crime of selling his Fish to a Man who gives a better price than

The island yoles had relatively large sails and were light in construction; although very seaworthy they were shallow and said to be very 'wet'. In this 1897 photo the 'fleet' is leaving South Harbour for the fishing grounds, some of which lay several miles offshore.

his monopolizing Landlord, no other proprietor of land will employ him, or allow him to settle on his land. This association among the Gentlemen must check the spirit of the people, and benumb their exertions.'

On Fair Isle this oppressive regime was introduced when the island was owned by the Sinclairs of Quendale, continued throughout the period in which the Stewarts of Brough were lairds, and was carried on by the Bruces of Sumburgh from the time John Bruce acquired the island in 1866 until finally dealt a death blow by the passing of the Crofters Act

31

20 years later. By then the findings of the 'Truck' Commission of Enquiry held in 1872 had been well publicised. The evidence relating to Fair Isle presented to that Enquiry included statements claiming that the value given for fish was lower there than on the mainland while meal, tea, sugar, cotton and other goods taken to the isle were very highly priced; all trading with outsiders was prohibited, except for eggs and hosiery; and the islanders were bound to work only for the proprietor. Among those giving evidence were representatives of families driven from the isle to Orkney in 1869, after their menfolk had worked with the salvage squad on the *Lessing*.

Even the arrival of free-market conditions did not greatly help the isolated Fair Islanders. How and where could they market their catches, now that the responsibility for doing so lay with them alone? Nor was this their only problem. A gradual decrease in the size and number of tusk and ling in Shetland waters had been noted by Robertson as far back as 1769; a century later the 'haaf' (ocean) fishing for these species had been abandoned at Fair Isle and the fishermen had turned to saithe (coalfish — a relative of cod) which were abundant much closer inshore but were of lower market value. In the early 1880s Tudor recorded that 'about 90 to 100 tons of fish, principally saithe, are cured every year and some 50 barrels of oil made, of which about half is best-quality cod-liver oil. The saithe are mostly caught off the south end of the island in boats worked under sail.' But early this century the huge shoals of saithe also vanished, and by 1909-14, when the Duchess of Bedford was visiting the isle, there was apparently little, if any, commercial fishing going on.

There were still plenty of piltocks — half-grown saithe — to be had, however, and these continued to form an important part of the islanders' diet, fresh or salted and dried. With the return of the men who had been away during the First World War commercial fishing was resumed, this time mainly for haddock, which were salted and dried. By then the island was being served more or less regularly by packet-boat, so the problem of getting fish away to market was to some extent alleviated. But the islanders with their hand-lines could not for long compete against the steam trawlers which were now fishing ever closer to the island, though they did benefit from free hand-outs of fish from trawler skippers anxious not to be reported for fishing inside the three-mile limit! 'Friendly' trawlers also provided a means of sending island catches to market in Aberdeen and a source of damaged fish for baiting halibut lines and lobster pots.

Fishing for haddock and halibut continued until the late 1950s, by which time catches had declined to such an extent that the income no longer compensated for the time spent at sea and the cost of transport to

When not in use the yoles had to be hauled well above the high tide mark; for protection against winter's storms each was stowed into a dug-out 'noost'. The Viking design, pointed at both bow and stern, still predominated in 1936.

market. The last worthwhile season for halibut was 1959, when one boat caught eight fish. Today only one or two boats still go off at all regularly to fish, mainly for home consumption. Most of the ling, haddock, mackerel, piltock and (rarely) cod caught are eaten fresh or put in the deep freeze, but some haddocks and piltocks are still dried for winter use, and a few lobsters are exported, nowadays by air. Fishing, which once governed life on Fair Isle, is currently little more than a recreational pursuit — and nobody on the isle today has first-hand experience of the physical hardships associated with the past dependence upon fishing from small boats.

For survival in Fair Isle's stormy waters, a small open boat must be extremely buoyant and manoeuvrable. It is a tribute to the design skills of the Vikings that in the centuries that have passed since they first brought their boats across the sea from Norway there has been little change in the overall shape of the yoles typical of Dunrossness and Fair Isle, although the latter is slightly longer and narrower than the 'Ness yole'. Tudor commented that 'These boats are at the present day peculiar to the island, and, to a stranger, seem awful cockle-shells. They are, however, said to be very buoyant, though, as can well be imagined from their make, very 'wet'. In spite of their wetness the natives refuse to change to larger boats, as they consider their own more adapted for the furious tideways in which the island is situated.'

Tudor details the measurements of a typical Fair Isle yole: over all, 22ft 9in; depth amidships, 1ft 9in; extreme beam (breadth), 6ft; stem and stern alike (ie pointed at both ends); mast, 16ft, with 14ft 6in hoist (for the sail). The sail was square and had tremendous lifting power, giving the yole a good turn of speed with a following wind. Suppleness, for coping with choppy seas, and lightness, for ease in hauling up to the safety of their sheltering noosts, were all-important, and came from the shallow yet stream-lined shape and the light, clinker-built shell of broad, over-lapping planks. As in all Shetland boats, the oars pivot against an upright wooden peg, which serves as a rowlock, and are secured to the gunwale with a loop of hide or rope. This system means that, when necessary, the rower can ship his oars without risk of them being lost overboard.

When Patrick Fotheringhame visited Fair Isle in 1804 he reported that 'There are at present on the island eighteen fishing boats in each of which three men are usually employed. Several of these are however almost unfit for service, and the inhabitants are much in want of a supply. Three or four more could be employed if they could be got. These boats are usually brought from Norway by the proprietor . . . .'. Although many of the Fair Isle boats were imported from Norway — in a dismantled form, like a present-day furniture kit — some were built on the island, though all the timber required had to be brought in. After an interval of some 30 years, an island-built boat was again present in 1988, when a young islander, having completed his apprenticeship in Norway, returned to build and launch his first boat, appropriately named *Alpha*.

Not surprisingly, bad weather did sometimes overwhelm even the very seaworthy island yoles, and over the years a number of Fair Islanders were lost in this way. Such disasters were just as likely to occur when the boats went off to barter with passing ships as when they were out fishing. In September 1897, for example, 'Four skiffs set out to barter vegetables, poultry and hosiery with passing vessels, fifteen of which were sailing eastward past the island. Towards evening the weather changed; the wind began to blow very hard from the north-west . . . Two of the skiffs fortunately made land before dark, but the other two were missing the whole night. Early next morning one of the missing boats was noticed from the heights. When the craft was reached it was found that of the seven occupants only three were alive, and they were exhausted and in a helpless state.' No trace of the other boat was ever found, and the disaster left four widows and 27 dependants unprovided for.

As bartering and fishing declined in importance so too did the risk of death by drowning, but the last such loss was as recent as 1961, when a lobster boat overturned off the Nizz, below the North Light, throwing the crew of three into the water. The most experienced crew member managed to get his teenage nephew ashore and guide him up the cliff to safety, but the boat's owner was trapped beneath it.

In addition to a boat-design unique to the island, the Fair Islanders also developed their own style of tub for storing fishing lines so that they did not get tangled. The long-lines used for the haaf fishing, and later for haddock and halibut, had short side-spurs, known as tomes and at one time made from pony tail hair, fastened to them at regular intervals. As each tome carried a hook, and the line had to be fed over the side smoothly as the boat moved forward, the need for an efficient anti-tangle system is obvious. With the lines coiled in the centre and the hooks arranged tidily and in sequence round the rim, the Fair Isle line tub served its purpose well. Limpets, or pieces of herring or mackerel, were the usual bait on haddock lines, and piltock heads or side-cuts on the big halibut hooks. Piltocks, and the smaller-sized saithe known as sillocks, were often caught by 'craig fishing' with hand lines from the rocky shore. Probably the oldest technique on the island and originally the main means of catching fish for home consumption, craig fishing is still in use today. The limpets needed for bait are levered off the rocks and heated in a pot of water until they come easily from the shell. When old George Stout of Field fished regularly in the North Haven in the 1960s he usually chewed them before use (to soften them) and often 'sprooted' or spat some onto the water to attract the fish.

The prospects of success in both haaf and halibut fishing depended greatly on the fishermen's skill in locating the best fishing grounds. Knowledge of these was handed down from one generation to the next, using a system of bearings on prominent landmarks, known on Fair Isle as 'fishing hands'. As the boat was rowed out to sea, watch was kept for the moment when two stacks or headlands some distance apart could be seen at the same time, or two features could be lined up — like markers at the entrance to a harbour. Many of the hands sound like a foreign language, for example 'Luistemil', where light can be seen between a rock and the face of Malcolm's Head. One of the best halibut grounds, far offshore, was located by 'Engan Ru an' Huggie Little' — when a particularly red patch of rock on the high face of Sheep Craig and a prominent ridge on the west side of Malcolm's Head are both visible. Similarly, when Glimster, a rocky point on the north-west corner of the isle, is either 'dipping' or 'coming', vanishing from or coming into sight, the crew knows that the *Good Shepherd* is about 10 miles from home.

Limpets or pieces of piltock (carried in the straw 'kishie' in the foreground) were used as bait, and the islanders had their own design of line-tub, with the numerous hooks of the long-lines tidily arranged round the edge so that they did not become entangled.

Every recognisable stack, skerry, geo and headland around the coast is named, so the hands provided an easy and reliable way of finding the same patch of sea on successive trips. Familiarity with the hands was not enough, however. The fishermen also had to know how the tides ran and be able to estimate the rate at which the boat would be carried off course at different states of the tide.

In 1959, when I was fortunate enough to be taken out in one of the Fair Isle boats (despite the fact that it is traditionally considered unlucky even to meet a female when you are going fishing!), I discovered just how exciting it can be to catch a halibut weighing 35-50 kilos, and measuring maybe 1½ metres long by one metre across. When we reached the fishing ground a buoy was thrown overboard and a large stone sinker or 'kappi', attached to the buoy by about 50 fathoms of rope, was lowered over the side. The main line, already fastened to the buoy rope and equipped with a piltock-baited tome every six fathoms, was then paid out; when all the line was shot, a second kappi stone and buoy were attached and put overboard. That done, the crew rested, as the boat wallowed in the swell, until the tide had turned and it was time for action again. At first there was suspenseful silence, apart from the creak of the oars, as we slowly retraced our path and the line was hauled in and neatly stowed, but suddenly came the cry of 'A 'but, a 'but' and all was immediately excitement. The oars were shipped and the 'huggie stauf' (gaff) seized in readiness; moments later the great flat shape of a large halibut came slithering in over the gunwale to lie flapping in the bottom of the boat. A successful trip — so I did not, after all, have to be thrown overboard as a penalty for bringing bad luck!

Work was by no means finished when the crews came ashore and hauled their boats up to safety well above the high-tide mark. The preparation and drying of the fish took about a month, and in the Truck System period the fishermen were themselves responsible for this work. After weighing by the proprietor's agent or factor, the fish were split and had part of the backbone removed. They were then washed and laid in layers in a vat of brine. After two or three days 'pickling' they were removed from the vat, washed again, allowed to drain, and then spread skin-side down on the man-made pebble beach at Skadan to dry. If it rained, the half-dry fish were built into temporary conical heaps and covered with tarpaulins. The spreading and stacking, much of which was done by young 'beach boys', alternated for several weeks until the fish were completely dry and stiff — at which stage they developed a phosphorescence which was visible at night from far out to sea and so bright that it occasionally caused passing ships to think that flares were being lit! When dry the fish, now weighing only half their original 'wet'

Halibut fishing provided useful income for some time after commercial catching of cod, ling and saithe had been abandoned, but it too became uneconomic around 1960. Problems with the storage and transport of fresh fish contributed to the islanders' inability to compete with full-time fishermen working from larger boats.

weight, were stored under cover until taken away in the merchant's sloop.

Coping with a catch of halibut presented different problems, mainly related to the speed with which it could be got to market, as halibut (and haddock and mackerel) cannot be satisfactorily dried. There was no deep freeze or cold store available on Fair Isle when halibut were being caught commercially, so fishing was restricted to times when the catch could be sent away on trawlers working in the vicinity or to the days which immediately preceded sailings of the *Good Shepherd*. The trawler skippers were generally willing to take the islanders' halibut, in ice, to Aberdeen market — a preferable transport route to the alternative of the crossing to Grutness, lorry to Lerwick, and south to Aberdeen on the *St Clair*.

Lobsters were somewhat easier to cope with, as they could be kept alive until they reached their destination. As one member of a lobster boat's crew lifted the pots and removed the catch, a second tied string round the lobsters' big claws and laid them in the bottom of the boat.

Today 'lobstering' is the only commercial fishing carried out on Fair Isle; the limited quantities taken are exported by air. In this shot the typical 'wooden pin' rowlocks, with a rope loop round the oar, are clearly visible.

Back in harbour, the lobsters were packed in crates and floated off the pier until 'boat day'. In the late 1950s and early 1960s they were then sent 'direct', ie via the *Good Shepherd*, lorry, *St Clair* and another lorry, to the canneries at Inverbervie, where they made 3/− a lb. More than 2,000 lobsters were dispatched in 1959, when catches were at their peak. Later, with the opening of a lobster pool in Shetland where the shellfish could be stored until air-freighted to London or the Continent, the islanders' responsibilities for transport were much reduced, though the freight costs were still considerable. With the closure of the Shetland pool lobster catching became uneconomic (not just on Fair Isle, but elsewhere in Shetland too), as haaf and halibut fishing had done earlier.

Today the importance, for Fair Isle, of the shoals of piltocks, their younger brothers the sillocks, and the sandeels which still swarm in the waters round the island, lies in the fact that they provide the growing populations of seabirds and grey seals with an abundant food supply. But changes are taking place even among these 'small fry'. The 1980s have seen up to nine large trawlers fishing near the island for sandeels, towing bagnets which scoop up thousands, or maybe millions, of these tiny fish at every haul. When the commercial sandeel fishing started thousands of tons a year were caught around Shetland, to be processed into fish-meal or frozen and exported for feeding to mink in Scandinavia; more recently catches have been declining but the fishing goes on. Concern has been expressed that this intensive harvesting may result in a slump in the sandeel population, as has happened with other species in the past. Heavy mortality among young seabirds on the isle in 1988 increased this concern and led to renewed demands that action be taken to determine whether over-fishing is, in fact, responsible for fluctuating fish populations — in which case greater control of inshore fishing will be needed — or whether such fluctuations are due to changing sea temperatures and other factors, not yet fully understood.

One thing seems certain, however: in future the productivity of the sea is likely to be of much greater importance to Fair Isle's seabirds than to the island's human inhabitants. Increasing competition and changing market demands have ended the islanders' long tradition of fishing as a livelihood and it may never again become economically viable — even if the construction of a breakwater should make it possible to operate larger boats in greater safety. Fortunately, however, as the harvest of the sea has declined the productivity of the land has increased.

CHAPTER FOUR

Labouring on the Land

Over the last three centuries crofting on Fair Isle has changed only slowly, with occasional spurts when circumstances favoured particular types of development. Poor communications have been a major factor in delaying agricultural progress, and still affect the practicalities and economics of livestock production, while climatic conditions will always limit the options for crop growing. But two of the principal earlier constraints on improvement, insecurity of tenure and lack of capital, are no longer such serious problems, thanks to crofting legislation and the introduction of grant aid.

Since island land-use was first documented in detail there have been several notable changes in the distribution and size of the crofts, while the balance between cattle, sheep and ponies has varied widely over the years. Right up to the end of World War II, however, crofting techniques were basically the same as they had been for many generations. Oxen were still in use on some crofts in the early 1950s, and cultivation and harvesting was mostly done by labour-intensive methods. It was only in the 1960s that the introduction of new techniques started to accelerate, and in the late 1980s that large-scale improvement of the common grazing — the scattald — was attempted for the first time. As in nearly all aspects of island life, co-operative effort has been an essential ingredient in achieving progress.

For most of the historic period Fair Islanders' lives were governed largely by their landlords, with the crofters often struggling to find the rent (usually paid in kind) demanded by the laird, as well as trying to feed themselves and their families. Under the Truck System life was even harder; crofts were sub-divided, because more families meant more men available to fish for the laird, leases were shortened — often to less than a year — and without security of tenure there was no incentive to improve either land or buildings. Land improvement would have been difficult anyway, as only the kailyards (garden ground) near the houses had stock-proof boundaries and the 'inbye' land was managed on the run-rig system, with each croft cultivating several small, scattered strips of ground and the livestock free to roam at will for much of the year. That all suitable ground was at one time under cultivation is clear from the still-detectable signs of old field systems.

The 38 crofts occupied in 1829 were clustered in four townships, Shirva, Leogh, Gaila and Busta, which appear on the earliest detailed map of Fair Isle, dated 1839 (see Map 1). That map also shows isolated houses at Setter (now Vaasetter) and Taing and ruins in the vicinity of Field and Barkland; these were perhaps the 'few outsets not long occupied' referred to in the New Statistical Account of 1841 — new ground being brought into cultivation at a time of expanding population. The most northerly field systems identified by the Bradford University survey, at Vaasetter and between Finniquoy and Burn of Vatstrass, probably date from around this period. In 1845 individual holdings were formed by reallocating groups of rigs ('planking', from the Norse 'planka' — a field), which improved the situation from the farming angle but left 12 families virtually landless and several others with plots of only 2-2½ acres. The planking reduced the number of crofts to 31 and produced a scattered distribution pattern very similar to today's, but with landless families still living at the old township sites.

As the population continued to grow life became more and more difficult until, in 1862, a mass emigration took place; those who left included several of the families who had been struggling to survive virtually without land. Five new holdings were created in 1924, for the benefit of men who had returned from the war, and fifteen crofts were again enlarged. The changes that have taken place since then have been only minor ones, involving reallocation of inbye ground and division of previously shared rough grazings.

Security of tenure and the right to compensation for improvements came towards the end of last century with the first Crofting Act, which also provided for the determination of fair rents. Complaints that Fair Isle rents were too high were apparently valid, as a visit by the Crofters' Commission in 1892 resulted in an average reduction of 22%. By the time rents were next reviewed, by the Land Court in 1946, many new byres, barns and other outhouses had been built, drains dug and new fences erected. Despite these improvements, and the general increase in agricultural values at that time, rents were again reduced. In the Court's view the failure of the fishing industry, the island's isolated position, and the difficulties of transport had, since 1892, combined to change the situation on Fair Isle from that of a 'more or less self-contained and self-

Shepherding the Sheep Craig flock often involved retrieving sheep that tried to retain their freedom by jumping down to a ledge below the rim of the cliff. With the final removal of the flock such hazardous operations became unnecessary.

supporting community' to one which was 'a most precarious and unattractive proposition'. On a lighter note, the Court also suggested that action might be taken against one crofter, whose over-numerous sheep regularly trespassed on his neighbours' ground, under the Winter Herding Act of 1696! The records do not show whether the accused did suffer 'poinding of trespassing stock and the imposition of penalties' – but he did continue to keep more sheep than his land could feed.

Although most of the inbye land has only been fenced within the last 30-40 years, some parts of the island were enclosed much earlier. Nobody knows when the first 'feelie' (turf) dyke separating hill and inbye ground was built – perhaps long before 1750, when its presence was first recorded on a map. At that time it ran diagonally across the isle, from Gunnawark to Hesswalls. Its western section, with a pronounced dog-leg kink, can still be seen but most of the eastern part, which passed close to the croft then known as Setter, has vanished as a result of cultivation. A second turf dyke was constructed, possibly quite soon after the isle was surveyed in 1839, to be replaced in turn by the present stout stone dyke. The hill dyke is shown as part-built on the 1878 OS map – two straight lines not far north of the feelie dyke but at varying distance from it, with a wide gap still to be filled in the middle; that final section included the 'lay-by' giving access to the rocket station.

The very first stone dyke built to keep sheep in (as opposed to kailyard dykes keeping stock out) appears to be the one still standing at the North Haven, for the 1841 Statistical Account records that Buness, which is now part of the common grazing, was 'fenced with a high stone dyke across the isthmus' and grazed by a flock of 'south country sheep' (presumably Cheviots and possibly part of the proprietor's flock). The rectangular stone enclosure on Buness was probably used as a sheep pen and may date, at least in part, from the same period. Most, if not all, of the common grazings south of the hill dyke – Hoini, Malcolm's Head, The Rippack and Brecks – had boundary dykes or fences by the end of last century. The short L, Y or X-shaped walls which today provide shelter for sheep on the inbye land are thought by the Bradford archaeologists to mark the sites of former dwellings or barns, where a supply of stone would be readily available.

During the 19th century the rights to the common grazings, which had earlier been unregulated, were allocated between crofts by 'souming' or dividing into shares which represent the grazing for a set number of sheep. No croft had shares on all the areas and the number of shares on the scattald varied between crofts. In 1954, for example, the 679 acres of scattald carried 240 ewes, representing 30 shares, of which Shirva held five (40 ewes) and the other crofts from one to 3¼ shares. In 1959,

Although the fleeces of pure Shetland sheep can be 'roo'ed' (plucked free without cutting) most are now sheared. Judging by the expressions, work camp volunteers find this unaccustomed task a challenging one.

however, it was agreed that all occupied crofts should hold equal shares on the hill, as was already the case with the Buness and Vaasetter grazings.

Back in 1895 a meeting of crofters had been called 'for the purpose of finding out whether it is sheep or ponies that they intend keeping on the hill. Also finding out the marks to be used there' and the hill flock was 'numbered for the first time by the Fair Isle Hill Committee' the same year. The 'marks', an elaborate code of nicks and notches cut into the sheep's ears, had to be applied while the lambs were still young enough to be caught easily on the open hill. To achieve this meant that at lambing-time each crofter had to go round the area on which his ewes normally grazed, at least once a day — a time-consuming task for men with many other duties to perform. Not surprisingly, some lambs remained unmarked and the competing claims to these when they were gathered in for weaning inevitably led to dispute. In 1983, however, a more co-operative approach to management of the hill sheep was introduced; marking ceased and in autumn the lambs are now allocated to the different crofts by drawing lots.

The hill sheep are pure Shetland stock; small and hardy, they range in colour from white through the varying moorit (fawn-brown) shades and also through grey to black. Characteristic of the breed is its very fine, soft wool and the way in which the old fleece can be 'roo'ed' or plucked free from the current season's growth without the need for shearing. Characteristic too is the Shetland's goat-like agility, enabling it to graze apparently inaccessible grassy cliff-ledges and descend precipitous paths to feed on seaweed — habits which sometimes result in a sheep becoming stuck and having to be rescued. It was when a would-be rescuer slipped and had to be rescued himself that the islanders earned the Carnegie Hero Award displayed in the Community Hall.

Twelve men helped with that rescue in May 1956, which took place on a dark, wet night and on a cliff-face which had long been considered unscalable. By the light of a Tilley lamp three men roped down 200 feet of the sheer cliffs below Ward Hill to reach the ledge where the injured man lay with a badly broken thigh and secure him to a stretcher. While on the cliff-face both rescuers and rescued were in considerable danger from falling rock — and for some the job was not finished even when the stretcher had been hauled up to safety, as the patient then had to be evacuated without delay on the *Good Shepherd*. The Fair Islanders involved in this courageous rescue well deserved their bronze medallion, the highest award of the Carnegie Hero Fund.

Cliff-climbing in order to rescue a stranded sheep is bad enough, but for hundreds of years it was a routine operation in connection with the small flock kept on Sheep Craig, to which the only access is up the cliff on the seaward side. 'Sheep Craig hath very excellent grass and the sheep there are very fat', wrote Rev. James Kay. 'Men on foot catch them without difficulty for being chased but once about the Rock they fall of their own accord which if they do not, the shepherd concludes them not fat enough for slaughter'. When I accompanied the roo'ing party in the 1950s the sheep were not quite so obliging — or not quite so fat — and circled the summit several times before being cornered in a pen of rope-netting or collared with a flying tackle! Mutton from the Craig was regarded as the tastiest on the island, but this can have been small consolation to tenants of Stackhoull (alias Rock Cottage), who had no land other than 'the Rock'. Despite the risks involved in reaching the

Co-ordinated teamwork was essential when 'delling' with Shetland spades. At one time these spades, with small blades and a single foot rest, were the most widely used implements of cultivation. The croft in the background is Springfield.

flock, the income from it was so necessary that Sheep Craig was grazed almost continuously until 1977. Today there are easier ways of earning money — but it is hard to believe that the islanders' enthusiasm for cliff-climbing was ever sufficient to justify the notice erected in 1891: 'All Trespassers are strictly prohibited from trespassing on the Sheep Rock. Signed, John Bruce'.

Only the Sheep Craig flock was exempt from the legal requirement that dipping be carried out annually to protect against sheep scab. All the hill sheep, and also those on the inbye land — which now include a mixture of breeds, have to be brought to the 'crü' (the pens at the North Grind) and 'dunked' in a bath of dip. The dip tank is a relatively recent improvement; before it was built the operation was a somewhat inefficient affair with the dip being poured onto the sheep — which so amused the Duchess of Bedford that she 'took some photographs of the Fair Isle sheep dipping, as carried out with the blue enamelled teapot'.

Although sheep are now the only stock grazed on the hill this was not always the case; cattle, ponies and pigs once also ranged freely about the island. According to the Armada diarist 'They have some cattle, quite enough for themselves for they rarely eat meat. They depend upon the milk and butter from the cows.' The 'nearly 200 black cattle' recorded in the Old Statistical Account was possibly an over-estimate, but there were certainly 80-100 present in the early 19th century, and 30 were put up for sale by the 23 families that emigrated in 1862. Numbers were probably dropping by the turn of the century and were down to seven or eight in the mid-1950s, when there were few children on the isle and some people used tinned milk. They were privileged cows in those days, with a highly-subsidised Department of Agriculture bull kept for their benefit. Today artificial insemination is used, a development which became possible when deep-freezes allowed semen to be stored on the isle until required.

Fotheringhame's comprehensive report of 1804 made no mention of oxen, and it seems likely that Bruce introduced them as draught animals in the late 1800s, when road-building made it possible for carts to be used. During the first half of this century ox-carts were the main form of transport for bringing peats home from the hill and goods from pier to shop. Tediously slow but steady, the oxen took 3-4 hours to make the round trip from the village to the peat banks at Dronger and back. When the last ox was taken away about 1951 it suffered the indignity of being forced to swim from the North Haven shore out to a waiting drifter, which hoisted it aboard. Indeed until the construction of the deep-water pier and the arrival of the *Good Shepherd III* cattle-loading continued to be a problem.

Prior to the oxen period Shetland ponies were the beasts of burden, 'kept solely for carrying home peat' which was loaded into 'maeshies', straw baskets slung across the pony's back on a wooden pack-saddle. There were more than 80 ponies on Fair Isle in 1829 but by the end of the century few were left and these were used mainly for breeding, the young stock being exported for sale.

As for pigs, not many have been kept on Fair Isle since 1900 — which is perhaps strange when one considers how much more abundant food scraps are now than in the past. When Sir Walter Scott visited the isle in 1814 he noted 'pigs, fowls, cows, men, women and children all living promiscuously under the same roof', while a visitor some 60 years later commented 'You may find a pig luxuriously enjoying the hot ashes, hobnobbing with a dog, cat or lamb across the hearth'. With a total of 93 pigs present in 1829 it is clear that they cannot all have enjoyed such comfort; most presumably had to fend for themselves outside, rooting up whatever tasty morsels they could find on the hill and around the crofts. According to one writer the flesh of the Shetland swine was 'extremely delicious, the fat and lean being beautifully intermixed'. It seems a pity that such a tasty source of meat should have vanished from the island scene.

Even when draught oxen were available much of the cultivation work was still done by man — or woman — power, and scenes like this were common in the early part of this century. Behind the harrowers is one of the planticrubs used for protecting cabbage seedlings from wind and sheep.

In the days when the inbye land was cultivated under the run-rig system it was probably only the milking cows whose movements were restricted by tethering, the other stock being herded out of the growing crops in summer and enjoying free range in winter. The first step towards alleviating the damage and irritation caused by beasts wandering at will came in 1876 when 'by mutual consent of the tenants' it was decreed that 'all stock going through the Town lands' were to be tethered from 27 April to 23 October. James Anderson, who recorded this and many other island events in the diary he kept for more than 50 years, had come to Fair Isle as grieve to the Laird, John Bruce, and was involved in the development of Vaasetter as a 'model' farm. He had been preceded briefly by Peter McGregor, who is described as 'Farm Manager at Setter' in the 1875 record of his marriage 'by declaration in the presence of

W. Laurence, John Bruce JP and George Leslie'. McGregor's stay on the isle was apparently a short one, and it was Anderson who carried out most of the improvements at Vaasetter. These acted as a spur to other crofters, and led to a considerable increase in the area under cultivation and to new techniques gradually replacing practices which had been followed for centuries.

Early visitors to Fair Isle varied widely in their assessment of its fertility and the productivity of its arable ground. James Kay considered that 'ye most part of the Isle might be made good corn land', while Robertson claimed that 'the soil seems peculiarly fitted for barley of which a considerable quantity is annually exported to Shetland' – a statement which is hard to credit in view of the fact that the population at the time (1769) exceeded 200 and there were probably no more than 75 acres under cultivation. Comments such as 'arable land . . . of moderate fertility' and 'a good deal of meadow, tolerably productive of herbage', made by an agriculturist, are likely to have been more realistic. And the fact that 'the crops are . . . very precarious, owing to sea gusting' was pointed out by Fotheringhame, who also noted that 'the grain is seldom sufficient to support the inhabitants for one half of the year.'

Bere, a primitive form of barley, was probably first grown on Fair Isle in Norse times and remained the most important crop for hundreds of years. The shipwrecked Spaniards found the islanders 'without bread except for a few barley meal bannocks cooked over the embers of the fuel', and bere-meal was used for various other baked dishes as well as for the barley-meal equivalents of porridge and brose. Oats were also grown, at least from the 17th century, and were particularly valued for the straw, which was more suitable than barley straw for thatch and for making baskets, chairbacks, ropes and other essential items. Oats were sometimes used in the sheaf for cattle feeding, but were more often at least partly threshed first to remove most of the grain, usually by laying the sheaves on the barn floor and beating them with a flail but sometimes by striking the whole sheaf against a barred frame.

Cabbages and potatoes are the only crops other than grain and grass with a long continuous history on Fair Isle. Cabbages probably came first – a visitor in 1774 was told that 'the best Cabbages in the world' could be bought there – and have the distinction of being the only crop not adversely affected by salt spray. The first bad gale of autumn may flatten corn and blacken potatoes, but the cabbages continue to flourish. Just how important they once were can be judged by the number of 'planticrubs' still scattered about the isle. It was in these small square enclosures that the seed was sown, in soil enriched with ash and compost and protected from wind and sheep by the dry-stone walls. After an autumn and winter's growth the seedlings were planted out in kailyards near the crofts. Most of the planticrubs in Homisdale and elsewhere on the common grazings have long been abandoned, but a few of those around the crofts are still in use in the late 1980s.

Haymaking must always have been a trying task on Fair Isle, where damp-laden air and high winds frequently make drying and stacking difficult. Until seed-mixtures containing ryegrass and clovers were introduced during the model farm improvements at Vaasetter, the grass cut for hay would be a mixture of short — and sweet — naturally-occurring grasses and wildflowers which, when 'well-cured' in a fine summer, produced good fodder but not much of it. As this was the main winter feed it is hardly surprising that after a bad summer more stock than usual had to be sold off the island, while those retained were likely to be weak from malnutrition by spring. Nowadays haymaking has largely been replaced by silage-making, a method of conserving grass which is much less dependent upon the weather.

Fotheringhame recorded in 1804 that 'the arable land is chiefly laboured by the women, the men paying no attention to the culture of the land except when the weather is so boisterous as to prevent them from going a-fishing', and this dependence upon female labour apparently lasted for some time after the fishing industry had failed. The traditional method of cultivation was by 'delling' with the rather clumsy-looking Shetland spade. This was a surprisingly efficient method of turning the soil, though slow and laborious — and dependent upon teams of three or four working harmoniously together. Although the introduction of a plough was one of the first innovations at Vaasetter it took 30-40 years for ploughing to completely replace delling. Even when ox-ploughs were in general use, and indeed after the first 'iron horses' arrived in 1946, most of the other work on the arable land continued to be carried out by manual labour. Harrows were pulled with a rope round the shoulders — this could still be seen on one croft as recently as the 1950s — and corn was sown broadcast from a straw basket or 'kishie', and harvested with a scythe. Mechanised harvesting eventually reached Fair Isle in the 1970s, with the importation of a binder and a small threshing mill. But today comparatively little corn is grown; the time and labour involved can be more profitably used in other ways, the people are no longer dependent upon crops grown on the isle, and even foodstuffs for the livestock can be imported with comparative ease.

Although several times larger than in the last century, the Fair Isle crofts are still too small to maintain a family — but the islanders themselves have decreed that the number of crofts should not be allowed to drop below a minimum of 15. Any increase in income from the land is

The corn mills at Finniquoy were still in use when this photo was taken during the 1914-18 war, but have since become ruinous. Plans are in hand for their restoration, as part of the island's 'living history'.

therefore dependent upon greater productivity, rather than expansion of crofting units. An important factor contributing towards recent growth in crofting income has been the improvement in transport facilities. The deepwater pier, bigger boat and fortnightly summer trip to Lerwick have all made the handling of stock and heavy goods, such as fertilisers and machinery, easier and cheaper, putting island crofts on a more competitive basis with those of mainland Shetland. Whereas in the past lambs bought in the isle by a dealer might be resold only days later at a substantially higher price, they can now be taken right to market at a cost (in 1988) to the crofter of only about 12p per head for transport from Fair Isle to Lerwick. Ewe subsidies and rising prices for lamb have also helped, as have improvements in management, which have substantially increased the number of lambs reared.

Advice from the College of Agriculture, together with grant aid under the Crofting Acts, has led to extensive liming and reseeding of the inbye land, with the long-neglected croft of Field now serving, as Vaasetter did in an earlier age, to demonstrate just what can be achieved by modern methods. The island is self-supporting in milk, and vegetables are produced for sale to the Bird Observatory. After much debate the Fair Isle Grazing Committee recently embarked upon a programme for improving the hill grazing; if this proves as successful as is hoped, it should be possible to increase both the size of the hill flock and its productivity. And, who knows, perhaps the Fair Isle cattle herd will also increase again in the years ahead.

As new barns and sheds were built, many of the old steading buildings vanished — either demolished or incorporated in the new — but several kilns and mills still survive to serve as visible reminders that home-produced meal once formed a major part of the islanders' diet. All the grain used for meal-making had first to be dried, by gentle toasting over a carefully-controlled fire set in the bottom of a kiln, and each croft had its own kiln, usually built onto the end of the barn; good examples can still be seen at Barkland, Shirva and Taft. Drying was followed by grinding; a 'knocking stane' (like a large pestle and mortar) or a rotating quern dealt with immediate needs or small quantities, but the bulk of the grain was taken to one of the small horizontal-wheeled 'click-mills' — so-called because two wooden parts strike each other at every turn of the millstone. Traces of the mills which once stood beside the Vaadal and Gilsetter Burns, and the dams and sluices that fed them, can still be seen. Those at the head of the Gill of Finniquoy, last used in the 1914-18 war, are being restored as part of the isle's programme for preserving 'living history', while examples of many implements that are now obsolete are displayed in the museum.

Crofting on Fair Isle has been transformed over the last 40 years and is still developing. But, whatever changes lie ahead, one thing is certain:

working the crofts will never in future be so demanding of man (and woman!) power as it was in the past. Which is just as well, since fewer hands are now available to carry out the many and varied tasks essential to the survival of an island community.

CHAPTER FIVE

Population Ups and Downs

In the five centuries that have passed since Fair Isle's inhabitants were first counted, the population has peaked at 380, in 1861, and dropped to an all-time low of only 42 permanent residents (excluding lighthouse families, nurse, teacher and Observatory staff) in 1973. For much of this period isolation and poverty were the principal factors affecting the islanders' lifestyle and only within the last 100 years have living standards risen markedly. Improvements in transport and amenities mean that in some respects Fair Isle now enjoys facilities comparable to many mainland situations, but the small size of the community continues to influence such matters as health care, education and pastoral care, though most of these too have improved greatly over the last 20-30 years.

Between 1588, when there were 17 households, and the late 18th century the population ranged from about 150 to 240, the main causes of decrease during this period being disasters at sea and at least one epidemic of smallpox. According to the Old Statistical Account the 32 families present in 1791 comprised 106 males and 114 females and included two individuals who were reputedly more than 100 years old. The writer of the OSA entry also commented 'as they live principally on bread and fish which it is admitted are very favourable to population, they have families as healthy as they are numerous'. Extended families of up to 14 individuals were then living in what can have been little more than hovels, with dry-stone walls, roofs of turf, and a central peat fire, and doubtless sharing their smoky accommodation with assorted animals. Like many other tasks, building a new house was a co-operative venture; 'the whole men of the island assembled and did the work without any remuneration but food'.

At times food was none too abundant. With a steadily expanding population crop failures could cause real hardship, and the isle, like many other communities, must have been grateful for the 'social security'

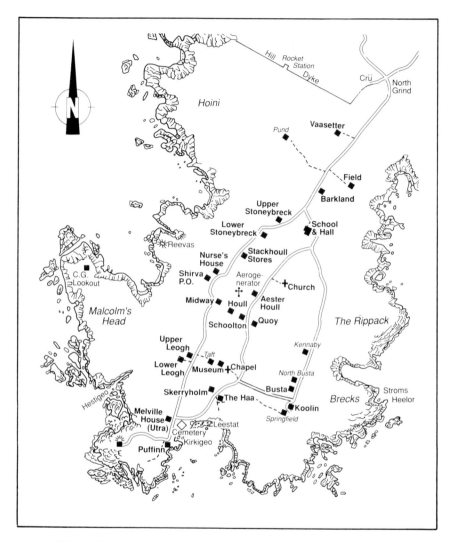

Map 2. The crofting area as it is today. Houses unoccupied in 1988 are named in italic type.

handouts of the day. In 1804 Shetland's distribution of 'charity meal and bread' included an extra 5 bolls of meal to the 260 Fair Islanders 'to make up for the considerable damage their share sustained in transport to Dunrossness and from thence to Fair Isle'. About 15 years later a visiting army officer commented 'the natives are in general half-starved . . . and have a look of savage apathy', and compared the Fair Isle situation unfavourably with that of Foula, where the population was almost static. So strong is the Fair Islanders' feeling for their homeland, however, that even in times of great hardship they are reluctant to leave.

Although badly stained, this old photo shows clearly the numerous straw ropes anchoring the thatch and encircling the chimney. Five one-window drystone houses of this type were still occupied in 1891; when new houses were built the old ones probably continued in use as barns.

The first recorded emigration took place between 1829 and 1841, when a few families moved to Orkney, reducing the population from 284 to 232. By 1861 numbers had risen again to 380 and there were reports that, owing to crop failure and a bad fishing season, the islanders were on the verge of starvation. As Chairman of the Poor Board for Dunrossness Parish, John Bruce (who was to buy the isle from Brough Estate a few years later) was involved in distributing money for the relief of the destitute and it was he who advised the islanders to take advantage of a fund available to help would-be emigrants. Twenty-three families eventually decided to take this opportunity of moving to a new life, where prospects should be better, and left for New Brunswick in May 1862.

Much had to be arranged in preparation for their departure, and Bruce, with the help of his son and the Fair Isle teacher, undertook most of the detailed organisation of this mass exodus. Passage to Canada was free and each adult would receive 10/− on arrival there, but the party needed transport to Glasgow; their cattle, ponies and other effects had to be sold; and funds were required for essential clothing and minor expenses on the journey. Bruce set up a subscription fund in Lerwick and the £16.4.0d raised was divided between the 23 families according to need. He also arranged for smallpox vaccination and, after a somewhat acrimonious correspondence with the factor in Orkney, organised transport from Fair Isle to Kirkwall on the Brough Estate sloop (named, ironically, the *No Joke*). From there the steamer took the party of 65 adults and 70 children south to Leith, where they were put on the train to Glasgow. Five weeks later they landed safely in St Johns, New Brunswick. According to contemporary reports they arrived 'all in good health and spirits', but for people who had seldom, if ever, been off the isle before, and had never visited a big city or seen a train, it must have been a traumatic journey. And for those left behind it was 'ane o' da blackest days I ever saw here'. Everyone had relations who had gone, one elderly lady parting with 32 first cousins, and there was little likelihood of ever seeing them again.

Life for those who remained on Fair Isle continued much as before. There was no immediate improvement in conditions when Bruce became the proprietor; indeed his prohibition on work being done for anyone but himself led to the departure to Orkney of another eight families. By 1871 the population was down to 224 and the houses were still primitive in the extreme, several of them without a single window. Though a proposal in 1874 for mass emigration to New Zealand came to nothing, several more families had gone by the end of the century, in some cases as a direct result of the 1897 boat disaster. By 1901 only 147 folk remained on the island — but at long last they were beginning to enjoy some improvement in their standard of living.

Until well on in the 19th century the Laird's residence, the Haa, was the only solidly-built house on the isle; its Orkney-style crow-stepped gables suggest that it was probably built during the period of Orcadian Stewart ownership. It was John Bruce the Younger who started to encourage the building of better croft houses, along with the agricultural developments he was introducing at Vaasetter. First he designed and had built a 'model' cottage, probably Barkland, which was constructed in 1879 for an incoming crofter whose name is perpetuated in Johnny Arcus' Park. Arcus and his Fair Isle born wife came to the isle from Orkney, which may explain why Barkland was roofed with Orkney flags; for the other croft houses Bruce supplied roofing slates, leaving the islanders to build the walls once an experienced quarryman had shown them how to 'convert rocks into stones'. Building must have proceeded at a good pace, as only five of the old one-window 'black houses' were still occupied at the 1891 census.

The new croft houses had three rooms ('but' and 'ben', and a small central 'closet' large enough to hold a box bed but little else), and a barn

House modernisation started with Midway (extreme right) having a second storey added and the Nurse's House (centre, unwhitened) an extension. The other houses are still basically as they were built in the 1880s, but with Stackhoull Stores extending the line of Rock Cottage. At that time (1959) the Post Office was in the small white barn in front of Shirva.

and kiln, byre and shed nearby. The 1881 plans for houses to be built at Stoneybreck, by George Irvine, and at Stackhoull, by Alex. Eunson, specified wooden floors in the 'parlour and closet', red pine for doors and windows, and all exposed wood to receive three coats of oil paint. The hearth was at the gable end, with a chimney in the thickness of the wall; cooking was done in black iron pots suspended over the peat fire. Many of the houses were wood-lined and fitted with doors which, like the roof and other timbers, had been salvaged from wrecks. The panelling in the Haa reputedly came from a single 80 foot log, which was towed across the Roost to be sawn into planks. And at Vaasetter discarded rocket sticks

The late 19th century houses had open hearths built into the gable end, with a chain to hold the kettle or cooking pot suspended inside the chimney. When the Queen visited Taft in 1960 she had tea beside a peat fire like this.

were gathered up and used to construct a false ceiling, on which dried fish could be stored.

Although a vast improvement on the old ones, these new houses still had their shortcomings. When the Duchess of Bedford rented Pund she confided in her diary 'When I am in bed with doors and windows closed, the wind blows my hair about and a strong breeze comes in all round the mantelpiece and where ceiling and walls nominally unite.' Apart from minor improvements, such as the addition of a porch or a 'back-house', most of these houses were to undergo little structural alteration until the 1950s-1960s. As recently as 1962 eight of the crofts still had no running water, only five had flush lavatories and just one had electricity. Since then all the houses that are currently occupied have been provided with 'mains' water, a bathroom and electricity, and most have been substantially enlarged.

As living conditions gradually improved so too did the health care available to the islanders. Apart from smallpox, the earliest recorded disease from which the Fair Isle folk suffered was a scaly skin condition, known as 'scald-head' and attributed by Kay to 'the distillations of the Fishes which hang above their heads as they enter the Skeos', though a dietary deficiency seems more likely to have been the cause. The fact that the isle still had no regular medical service of any kind in the 1880s provoked Tudor to advise visitors against landing 'without a pocket enema, as alteration in diet, and what not, are apt to bring on violent constipation'. Only five years previously a visiting minister had become ill and died before the doctor from Lerwick could reach him, the steamer on which the doctor was travelling having failed to locate the isle in mist. As recently as 1949 there was a similar incident, though with a happier ending, when stormy weather prevented the evacuation to hospital of an urgent maternity case and the surgeon coming to assist was so violently tossed about in the lifeboat that he broke his ankle. The baby fortunately arrived safely without his help.

Towards the end of the 1800s the isle was suggested as a suitable site for a sanatorium, which was ironic in view of the fact that tuberculosis was common — a situation that was hardly surprising, given the very poor housing, the overcrowding and the lack of sanitation. At least one consumptive young islander was nursed in the Duchess of Bedford's private hospital at Woburn, and nearly as many of the young men who went to the 1914-18 war died of tubercular meningitis, or measles, as of wounds. Infrequent contact with the outside world meant that the islanders had little resistance to infection, so that any common school-age complaint, once introduced, was likely to become an epidemic, affecting all age groups. In the first half of this century there were outbreaks of whooping cough, scarlet fever, mumps, chicken pox, measles and even jaundice, the last closing the school for a month in 1906. With more regular comings and goings serious epidemics became fewer, but in 1965 flu laid low all but one of the *Good Shepherd*'s crew, disrupting the boat's schedule.

During the 19th century it was usually the teacher who had to cope with any illness or accident as best he could, making use of the community medicine chest, but in 1903 a resident nurse arrived on the isle and for the first time trained assistance was available on the spot — perhaps especially valuable for midwifery cases, which shortly before had been described as 'often sadly mismanaged'. This first nurse, Ethel Payne, and those who succeeded her at usually annual intervals until the local authority District Nursing Service took over around 1915, was a Queen Victoria Jubilee Nurse. In order to qualify for the services of a Queen's Nurse, a Fair Isle Nursing Association had to be established, and the necessary funds assured. Initial financing came from the Disaster Fund set up for the dependants of those lost in the 1897 boating accident, and further help came from Mr James Coats of Paisley, whose visit to the island in his yacht at the turn of the century resulted not only in gifts of books and musical instruments but also in a supply of free medicines and dressings. With little ready money available, the islanders had great difficulty in finding their share of the nurse's modest salary, and paid her partly in kind; a letter written by Nurse Kelso soon after her arrival in 1908 records her horrified reaction when presented with a live chicken! Money contributions averaged 5/– per family in 1912 and the Northern Lighthouse Board gave £15. Visits by a doctor were rare and expensive — £20 a visit in 1909 — and most consultations were carried out by telegraph to a doctor in Kirkwall. For any specialist medical attention the patient had to travel to Lerwick and stay there at his own expense, a situation which still applies today in all except maternity and hospital cases.

Although Nurse Kelso and the other Victoria nurses stayed in the Haa, provided rent-free by Bruce, North Shirva became the official residence of the District Nurse, who was required to provide first aid, issue simple remedies and dispense health education — from premises which until 1957 lacked even such a basic facility as running water. The nurse's job in a small community like this may appear to be an easy one, with few regular patients requiring attention and a fairly 'flexi' time-table, but it carries unusually heavy responsibilities. Her diagnosis and decision may well tip the balance between life and death; a doctor at the other end of a telephone line can never be as helpful as one at the patient's bedside and often only the nurse is in a position to decide whether or not a case

The Haa, residence of the laird or his factor, is the oldest house on the isle. It had probably changed little, at least externally, between 1814, when Sir Walter Scott dined there, and 1936, when this photo was taken.

The nursing service established in the early 1900s brought a big improvement in the care of mums and babies — but laid a heavy responsibility on the nurse. This nurse (believed to be Nurse Mackenzie) probably supervised the birth of most, if not all, of the infants pictured with her.

should be treated as an emergency.

At a time when most Scottish schoolchildren were having regular medical and dental examinations those on Fair Isle only occasionally saw either doctor or dentist. Periodic visits to vaccinate the children were made from the late 19th century, and Nurse Mackenzie took the precaution of learning how to pull teeth before coming to the isle in 1911, but the 1915 instruction that the District Medical Officer was to visit the isle once a quarter was easier to set down than to carry out. The first visit by a dentist, in 1930, was apparently limited to talk and an issue of sweets! From 1937 to 1945 the children were medically examined on only three occasions, and when a dentist was persuaded to visit in 1948 he found that more than half the islanders required treatment. In one day he attended nine patients and took out 33 teeth. Since then the situation has improved greatly — provided that you manage to synchronise your toothache with the dentist's annual visit (complete with drills and dental chair), failing which you either endure or make the trip to Lerwick at your own expense.

A major factor in improving health-care provision has undoubtedly been the introduction of an air link with Shetland. This allows the doctor to make regular two-monthly visits in summer without having to spend more than a few hours of his time, but even more importantly it means that quick and comfortable evacuation to hospital is possible in all but the most difficult weather conditions. The possibility of an air ambulance service was suggested as far back as 1945, and the need for one was reiterated at frequent intervals during the 1950s and highlighted at the time of the 1956 cliff accident. But although the war-time airstrip was available there was no suitable small plane based within reach of Fair Isle until Loganair's Orkney inter-island flights started in 1966. At last the long hoped for air ambulance service became a reality, with the first emergency evacuation taking place in 1967. In the first seven months of 1988 there were no fewer than five ambulance flights, including two night-time ones with the runway marked by paraffin flares. Even Tudor would no longer need to come armed with his own emergency treatments if he were to visit the island today!

Changes were taking place, too, in church and school. Although their degree of inter-dependence has varied with time, religion and education have been closely linked on Fair Isle for more than 250 years. The first school was established by the Scottish Society for the Propagation of Christian Knowledge, a charitable body set up in 1709 and still active today, while in recent times the roles of teacher and missionary have often been either combined or shared between husband and wife. Over the centuries both church and school have moved several times, the earliest sites now being remembered only through place-names, and both institutions have benefited on occasion from salvage rewards and generous donations from well-wishers. That both (or rather all three, as there is a Methodist Chapel as well as a Kirk) are in as good condition as they are today is, however, largely due to the efforts, both physical and persuasive, of the islanders themselves.

Only a tradition survives to indicate the whereabouts of the early church building believed to have been situated at Kirkalees near Shirva, and it is impossible to say whether Kay was referring to it or to the later one above Kirkigeo when he wrote in the 1680s 'There is a little church here, more formally plenished and orderly frequented than will be easily believed.' The 'reader' responsible for 'catechising' the congregation in those days was doubtless the equivalent of the missionaries who followed him, authorised to preach the gospel and provide pastoral care but not to conduct weddings or celebrate the sacraments of communion and baptism. An ordained minister from Dunrossness usually visited the isle once a year, staying for two or three weeks and dealing with all matters that fell within his jurisdiction — which often involved him in a pretty full programme. On Rev. John Mill's first visit he preached 19 times in 20 days, and during two weeks in July 1793 he examined the Charity School and all the young people of the isle on the principles of religion, preached twice every Sabbath day, ordained four elders, rebuked and dismissed from discipline two delinquents, distributed money to the poor and baptised nine children. In 1828 no fewer than 22 were baptised together after the isle had had no ministerial visit for four years.

Although in 1804 the church was 'almost an entire ruin, being destitute of a roof and the seats mouldered and decayed by the admission of the rain', it was presumably still in use as John Irvine, Catechist, claimed the following year that every Sabbath afternoon he gave 108 young people religious instruction, from which they were 'profiting very well'. Whether a new building was erected or the old one re-roofed is not clear, but 'Da Auld Kirk' was certainly at the Kirkigeo site from pre-1839 to near the end of the century; its ruinous walls are now incorporated into the boundary of the present graveyard. The Presbyterian church in use today was built in 1892, by which time Fair Isle had a well-established tradition of a truly ecumenical approach to religion.

Methodism was introduced to the isle in 1825, by a young fisherman from Orkney, and within 15 years some 50 islanders had joined the Methodist Society. To begin with meetings were held in cottages but by 1862 the congregation had built its first chapel, at the site of the present one (which dates from 1885). Four generations of Wilsons served as lay preachers in the chapel; Stewart Wilson, the first of the line, completed 50 years of service and died actually in the pulpit. Although rather more than half the island families are by tradition Church of Scotland members, it has long been customary for all who can to attend both church and chapel services, which are held alternately — a very practical demonstration of ecumenism which often surprises visitors. As one international work-party put it 'We found the system of worship enlightening, with Methodists and Presbyterians worshipping shoulder to shoulder at each others' services'. Also impressive is the islanders' singing which was described in 1865 as 'lusty, with a not unpleasant wild, wail-like cadence' and in the 1930s as showing 'a fervour and strength which would put our languid southern congregations to shame'.

The archives of the Scottish Society for the Propagation of Christian Knowledge record the establishment of a school on the isle as long ago as August 1731, when 35 boys and 24 girls were enrolled, but, apart from the fact that it was at Gaila, near the Haa, little is known about that first school. If the Old Statistical Account can be believed, almost all the islanders could read and many could write by 1795 — a standard of literacy well above the average in the highlands and islands at that time.

Educational provision was not always as good as it might be, however, and when an inspector visited in 1824 he found the school in disrepair and the schoolmaster/catechist teaching in the church and his own house. There is no record of when the school moved to the site now occupied by Schoolton croft, but it was certainly there by 1839.

Matters not essential to keeping body and soul together probably received scant attention in the mid-19th century, when the population was increasing rapidly, Stewart of Brough was reputedly threatening to evict all his tenants, and arrangements were being made for the mass emigration. A new teacher/missionary, named Johnston, arrived in 1862, just in time to vaccinate the emigrants, and found the schoolhouse in such a poor state that he wrote 'It will be utterly impossible for me to remain here if I do not get a better house'. His predecessor, James Cheyne, had reared a family of nine there, so had presumably been more tolerant! Johnston must have carried out his threat, as three years later a party of Church of Scotland ministers visiting the isle found the school building 'dismantled, part of the roof off . . . The sole occupant a hen perched comfortably on a joist', and the islanders expressing great anxiety for the resumption of school work. The erection of 'a suitable schoolhouse' was one of the first works set in hand by Bruce after he acquired the island, so 'Da Auld Schule' was probably built in the late 1860s. It was there that William Laurence, who played such an important part in introducing life-saving apparatus and a regular mail service, took up his duties in 1875. Four years later, for his combined roles of missionary and teacher, he received a salary of £80 from the SSPCK.

Laurence's term of office spanned the transfer of responsibility for schooling to a parish School Board, under the 1872 Education Act which made education compulsory for the first time. Those entitled to vote for School Board members were 'all proprietors and tenants of and over £4 value on the roll in 1876' — which amounted to 20 islanders and John Bruce. The Board was responsible for the construction of the present school and schoolhouse. Although these buildings did not come into use until 1882, Fair Isle's 'Board School' celebrated its centenary in 1978 with the publication of a booklet comprising extracts from the school log and contributions from pupils past and present. This fascinating record illustrates the major educational developments during this period — and also gives insights into the lives of both pupils and teachers.

This century the roll reached its peak of 43 in 1900, dropped into single figures for the first time in 1941, and was down to two in 1951. Numbers did not exceed ten in the 1960s and early 1970s, but crept into the teens again in the late 1970s. At present, in 1988, there are 12 children attending the Fair Isle school. In the early days truancy following

Today all mothers-to-be leave the isle well in advance of the date the baby is due, making the journey to and from hospital in Lerwick both quickly and comfortably by air. This infant was an addition to the family of Roderick Thorne, the teacher who started the island's newspaper 'Fair Isle Times'.

Nowadays exchange visits with schools from distant parts of mainland Britain
— not to mention TV — give Fair Isle's schoolchildren a much wider
appreciation of the 'outside world' than their predecessors ever had. This group
includes a party from 'overseas'.

a wreck occurred frequently, punishment was administered with a length
of halibut line — and the school water closets were not used because
'there is no need for such in an open place like Fair Isle'. And from being
excited by the visit of an excursion steamer in 1896 the children have
progressed to taking in their stride air-tours of Shetland, exchange visits
with mainland schools and the winning of a national competition for
school newspapers.

In 1927 the first island child went on to secondary school in Lerwick,
but this did not become usual for nearly 30 years, and even then the
parents could opt for their children to remain at school on the isle until
they reached the age of 15. Since 1955 all secondary-age pupils have, in
fact, gone to Lerwick, with resultant long separations from their families,
though term-time visits home are now much more feasible than in the

days when there was only a once-weekly boat. As increasing numbers of young islanders went south for vocational training in the 1960s and 1970s they did so amid doubts as to whether they would ever return to live on Fair Isle, doubts which fortunately were to prove unfounded.

Early this century the Duchess of Bedford wrote of the Fair Islanders 'They appear to produce hardy annuals or biennials until they have a crop of at least six or eight' but by the end of the 1914-18 war the crofting population was declining steadily and in 1945 it was down to about 60. By then not only had the birth-rate decreased, it was also showing a marked imbalance between the sexes; 15 boys were born between 1935 and 1950, but when Edith Ann Stout arrived in 1953 she was the first baby girl born into an island family for 21 years. Whatever the reason for it, this imbalance effectively reduced the chance of marriage between cousins, which had been difficult to avoid in the days when the community was virtually self-contained. In future Fair Isle would be much more dependent upon 'new blood' from outside than it had been in the past.

Between 1850 and 1950 the pendulum had swung from a situation of gross overstocking, leading to destitution and emigration, to one in which the population was no longer either self-sufficient, in the sense of being able to maintain essential services such as the mailboat, or self-sustaining. Even after the establishment of the Bird Observatory had brought a new surge of optimism, the possibility of evacuation continued to loom ever nearer and morale reached its lowest ebb in the mid-1950s. Modern technology might be able to make life less dependent upon man-power but it alone could not ensure that the island would continue to support a resident population — a social life acceptable by modern standards is also essential for a viable community.

D

CHAPTER SIX

The Social Scene

Island dwelling obviously limits opportunities for many aspects of social life, for example by forcing the community to rely heavily on its own resources for entertainment and by restricting purchasing choice. In the days of the Truck System there was no choice at all over the purchase of goods, you bought what the laird's man had on offer or did without, and you paid his price, whether in money or in kind. Life in those days was a struggle for survival and there would be little time to spare for entertainment and little opportunity for getting to know anyone from outwith the island. Even in the early 1900s, although living conditions were becoming easier, Fair Isle folk had so little contact with 'outsiders' that the scope for choosing a marriage partner was generally limited to those living on the isle — a situation reflected in the fact that in the 1920s five brothers and a sister married five sisters and their brother!

Isolation imposed other practical problems, too, until well into the present century. Traditionally Fair Isle, like other country communities, looked after its own poor, but this was not easy in a situation where everyone was living at bare subsistence level and there was only one 'heritor' in a position to help financially. During the period 1828-41 the Kirk Session's minutes record payments of 5s 'to Laurence Leslie — a poor' and 3s 4½d 'to Wm. Williamson — a cripple', out of an available total of £2 14s 2¼d. 'Jacobina Wilson in Leogh' (perhaps a widow with children?) received a more generous 11s 7½d. In 1877 counter-claims by Bruce and 'A native of Fair Isle' appeared in the Orkney Herald; the first maintained that only two families were 'really poor' and that the factor had orders to supply them with all they required, to which the ex-islander replied that in the winter of 1875 'four men went through the island, two by two, to each house, and begged a little meat to keep them alive — judge how largely they are supplied out of the store'.

Elderly and infirm islanders continued to be supported solely by the

Fair Isle's first shop and Post Office were in Melville House, the only two-storey house built in the late 19th century. Both shop and PO have moved twice since this photo was taken, and telegraph poles have vanished from the scene as the wires have been put underground.

community, with presumably some help from the laird, until 1904, when small pensions became available to the oldest through the Strong bequest. William Strong (son of James, the tacksman at the time of Walter Scott's visit) had left the isle as a youngster and become a successful wine and spirit merchant. He left a legacy of £3,000 for the benefit of the islanders, but his family contested the will; when legal action eventually found in favour of Fair Isle the occasion was celebrated with a soiree in the old school.

It was only with the introduction of state old age pensions that all the elderly could be sure of a basic income. Even then things apparently did not proceed smoothly, for a typically bureaucratic reason. Although the Fair Isle pensioners put in their claims in good time, the officer concerned failed to reach the isle at the appointed date. He did get there eventually, but as his report was three weeks late the pensions were not paid. Appeals on behalf of the islanders received the response that 'owing to the geographical position of the island nothing more could be done'. Such problems are hopefully now a thing of the past, and today's pensioners not only receive their dues at the appropriate time but also have the chance of meals on wheels (supplied from the school kitchen) and sheltered housing.

Shopping opportunities started to improve in the latter half of the 19th century, when floating shops from Orkney and Shetland visited the isle occasionally, bringing groceries, boots and shoes, meal and other essentials. Among the earliest of these was *Summer Cloud*, designed for the job and built in Stromness; her first visit to Fair Isle was in May 1886, just a month after she was launched. A few years earlier, in 1878, a 20 ton packet boat, the *Deasil*, intended for both fishing and transporting goods, had been gifted to the islanders by the Society of Friends, but sadly proved of little benefit to them. There was no way of hauling her up in bad weather and she was not the responsibility of any particular person, so perhaps it was hardly surprising that, after being damaged on a trip to Orkney, she was left lying about until she fell to bits. Over the next 30 years no fewer than six more store-carrying packet boats, most of them Shetland-based, came to grief in the South Harbour.

The floating shops were a welcome addition to the less than adequate service provided by the laird — of which an islander commented to the Truck Commission 'There was always a shop but sometimes no goods in it'. It was sometime between 1871 and 1876 that the first real shop (as opposed to a barter store) opened, at Melville House, where the Post Office was also established in the late 1870s. To begin with Jerome Wilson, formerly of Schoolhouse (probably Schoolton) and already factor to Bruce, was in charge, but he was soon succeeded by an incomer, William Manson, one of 'Bruce's men'. It was he, presumably in his capacity as Registrar, who completed the 1891 census return, and recorded that he had a clerk and a grocer working under him. By the time Nurse Kelso arrived in 1908 the shop was at Leogh and under the charge of 'Old Tom' Wilson. The quality of Tom's stock was good, she reported, and there was usually plenty of it, although on one occasion, when there had been no mail boat for three months, he had nothing left but nails!

In 1946 the shop moved again, this time into a newly constructed building at Stackhoull, where it was run by 'Rock' Jimmy, so-called because the only land attached to his croft was the grazing on Sheep Rock (Craig). Following his departure a few years later the isle was left shop-less again for nearly seven years, and virtually all foodstuffs had to be ordered in advance from Dunrossness merchants. When Stackhoull Stores eventually reopened, in 1956, it provided work for the first family of incoming settlers — and the opportunity to buy fresh sausages, thanks to the installation of a paraffin refrigerator. Deep freezes followed in the early 1970s, and in 1986 the shop was extended to provide a much-needed public toilet.

Nurse Kelso considered that Old Tom's goods were 'as cheap as one

Oxen powered most of the island's transport from the late 1800s until World War II; conveying supplies from the North Haven pier to the shop, and carting home peats from the hill were their main tasks.

could get anywhere', but nowadays prices are inevitably affected by freight costs. As the *Scotsman* put it when reporting on a survey of food prices in 1976 'Prices in Fair Isle can be taken as the ultimate that should be found in a remote village or island, meeting all the conditions that cause high prices — small population, little passing trade, double trans-shipment of goods plus road transport, and the need to buy in small quantities at maximum trade prices and carriage costs.' Comparative prices in Aberdeen, Lerwick and Fair Isle were then: for a sliced loaf —

15p, 19p & 21½p; for 1lb butter — 31p, 36p & 50p; and for a large tin of peaches — 26p, 29p & 43p. There were some compensations, however, as Fair Isle had the cheapest milk and lamb in the whole of the UK, as it probably still has today.

Although an island shop can provide a fair choice of foods — especially now that deep-freezes are available — it clearly cannot also stock a comprehensive range of clothing, so mail order was making an important contribution to Fair Isle life long before it became as generally popular as it now is. As shopping for clothes became easier the fashion aspirations of the islanders rose and by the 1920s and 30s the girls were wearing smart evening gowns for the dances held in the Old School, by then the Village Hall. Now, with vastly improved air and sea links, it is actually possible to go out to Lerwick for a day and look before you buy — a luxury that earlier generations were never able to enjoy.

Despite improved communications and closer contact with the outside world, some aspects of social life have continued almost unchanged, for example the traditional 'lift', which involved families visiting each other for a social evening. The lift was probably the principal form of entertainment until relatively recently and is said to have originated with an annual celebration to mark the start of peat-cutting (or lifting), when a squad of men and women gathered early in the morning at a particular house, worked on the hill all day, and then spent the evening eating and chatting together as a group. Even after a hard day at the peats the women's hands would not be allowed to lie idle; the oil lamps gave plenty of light for spinning and knitting. The lift was, however, an occasion when the men did not work at making straw baskets and chairbacks, but simply reminisced or played cards.

It would be during such social evenings that folk tales were passed down from one generation to the next: tales of trowies (trolls), guid-folks (fairies) and mermaids, for example, and also stories of narrow escapes at sea and heroic rescues. One of the best-known of the trowie tales is the story of Grotti Finnie, an unpleasant monster with great horrible scaly hands and nasty curly nails, and one of the most popular poems is 'The muggie and the soo', which tells the story of a pig's battle for a stuffed fish stomach (a dish similar to a haggis). There were other things to be handed on too, such as the 'cures' — including one involving snails — recalled by the elderly Wilsons at the Haa croft (now Skerryholm), when they were in their seventies. Among the items the Wilsons recorded were the following 'working' rhymes. The first encourages the cow to let her milk flow freely, making the task of the hand-milker much easier:

> Cussie coo lat doon dy mylk
> An doo sall get a goon o sylk;
> A goon o sylk an o silver tee
> If du'll lat doon dy mylk ta me.

The second rhyme points out that it is not the spinning wheel's fault when the driving band comes off, it is the spinner's own careless (uncanny) hand that is responsible.

> Peerie wheel rin an peerie wheel spin
> An peerie wheel cast da baand,
> It's no ithin da peerie wheel's wyte,
> It's dee ain uncanny haand.

These stories and poems would originally be told in the Fair Isle dialect, described as recently as 1949 as being almost purely Norn in its intonation and idiom, but even then probably much diluted with words and phrases introduced from mainland Scotland and elsewhere. Like other island traditions, the dialect is slowly vanishing, and many of the old words will be unintelligible to most of today's islanders.

Although they probably soon ceased to use their native dialect in everyday speech, the emigrant Fair Islanders scattered around the world frequently retained fond, if perhaps 'rose-tinted', memories of the isle and wrote nostalgically about it. The verse below was written early this century, probably in Glasgow; others have been sent home by exiles in Canada and New Zealand.

> Far away across the waters, lies the dear land of our birth,
> Scattered are her sons and daughters, far and wide o'er all the earth.
> Oft we dream, 'tis not surprising, of thy rugged rock-bound shore,
> Of thy towering cliffs uprising, mid the cold grey ocean's roar.
> Yet thy every mood so varied, doth our hearts but closer bind,
> To the Isle with none compared, and our friends we've left behind.

Musical instruments, including a pianola, were among James Coats' gifts in the early 1900s, but there were almost certainly fiddlers on the isle long before that. In the past the music which helped to jolly an evening along might be unexpected in style, as when Nurse Kelso was entertained to hymns played on a violin in strict polka time, but more recently Fair Islanders have become increasingly known for the quality of their contributions to musical events 'overseas'. Representatives of three generations have taken part in folk festivals in both Shetland and Orkney, in 1985 a party travelled to Faroe to play and sing, and folk groups from there and elsewhere have visited the isle. Several of the islanders compose tunes for fiddle or accordion, often to commemorate special occasions, such as a wedding or the launching of a new boat. The example below was written for the school's centenary celebrations.

Centenary March

Alec Stout

Other social activities that have survived the changing times include the winter highlight of 'guizing', which traditionally takes place on New Year's Eve and is enjoyed by adults as well as children. Fair Isle weddings still maintain their reputation as occasions of great rejoicing, in which everybody joins, though nowadays they seldom spread over more than two days. And of course dances are a regular feature of the social scene, with music provided by the local dance band, which currently comprises violins, accordions and guitars. Fair Isle dances are energetic affairs, with

The local band provides live music for dances in the new Community Hall, which affords ample space for several sets of the ever-popular Quadrilles. Badminton and other sports are also housed in the hall, and there are regular showings of video films.

Lancers and Quadrilles much in demand, as are many different versions of the waltz. One of the highlights of the evening is the local version of the Cumberland Reel; known as 'Sheep Hill', it bears a strong resemblance to the stampede of men and beasts at the hill gathering! Dances in the 1980s are very different from those of the 1950s; then there were so few young women on the isle that only in summer, when visitors were present, was it possible to have more than a single set on the floor for a square dance — and on occasion men were even reduced to dancing as ladies. Today, with plenty of young couples and teenagers around, the floor is again filled at the dances held in the Community Hall. Nowadays the energetic part of the evening may be preceded by the showing of a video film but, with TV available in every home, films

73

Specialised activities such as choral singing and dramatics are dependent upon the presence of an island-resident able and willing to lead them. This cheerful group maintained Fair Isle's reputation for enthusiastic singing under the guidance of the shopkeeper of the day.

are less of an attraction than in the days of the fortnightly Highlands and Islands Film Guild shows, which reached the isle in 1956.

Other social activities tend to wax and wane with individual enthusiasms. During the 1920s a Dramatic Club was started up, providing many islanders with their first opportunity to see a play; George Stout of Field was highly praised for his performance in the leading role of the first one staged. The early 1970s saw a flourishing choir, under the leadership of Stewart Wilson, the shopkeeper at that time; their rendering of excerpts from the Messiah deeply impressed visiting members of an International Voluntary Service party. Nowadays most social activities take place in the Community Hall, which is also the venue for the weekly knitwear demonstration and show, and for evening classes in such varied subjects as dressmaking and navigation, art and keep fit. A Sports Club caters for badminton, table-tennis and indoor bowls, with basketball for juniors, while in summer island footballers challenge teams from the Observatory and the workcamps. For this range of activities to be viable there must, of course, be enough active people in the community to support them — a situation which could not have been achieved had new people not come to settle on the isle.

When morale was at its lowest ebb, in the mid-1950s, there were seven young men in the 18-30 age group but not one unmarried woman of similar age. Of those seven, two emigrated to New Zealand, one was drowned and one remained single. The other three did manage to find brides — one was the island nurse and another the visiting dentist's assistant — but only one of the three couples settled on the isle. And with the children then at school on Fair Isle due to go to Lerwick for secondary education, and perhaps south for vocational training, the prospects for maintaining the population with mainly 'native' blood seemed poor. Action was clearly required.

The first effort to attract settlers to Fair Isle was made in 1956, when the National Trust for Scotland advertised for a couple to take over the shop. From the many applicants — the majority of whom were attracted more by romantic notions of living on an island than through any realistic appreciation of what that involved — a couple with three young children were selected as the most suitable. But integration into a close-knit community, and acceptance of the restrictions of island life, demand special qualities of adaptability and determination, a firm family bond, and good health. That first family was unable to meet the challenge and stayed only a few years, as did several of their successors over the next three decades. There have, however, been some notable successes among the incomers who had no 'blood connection' with the island. At present the Wheelers, who took over the derelict croft of Field in 1972 and transformed it into a productive unit, hold the record, closely followed by the Bests and the Murrays, who arrived on the isle a year or so later.

Settlers who have family links with the isle start off with the advantage of having a much clearer idea of what they are coming to, and consequently have a better prospect of 'fitting in', though not all in this category have stayed. One such family, Annie and Stewart Thomson and their three children, arrived in 1957, giving a welcome boost to both the population and its morale; Annie is one of the two island women who married lighthouse keepers in the 1940s-1950s and later returned to settle. But it has really been the determination of the younger generation to continue living on Fair Isle, even after they have spent some time enjoying the amenities of the mainland, that has given new hope for the future.

Of the 15 island-reared youngsters who went away to take some form of vocational training in the 1960s-1970s no fewer than eight are now established in crofts or jobs on the island; six of the eight are married, two

When this wedding group was taken, about 80 years ago, nearly all marriages were between couples already living on the isle and often related to one another. This situation changed as communications improved and it became easier to meet potential partners from elsewhere.

of them to girls who came to work at the Bird Observatory. Training in agriculture and carpentry, and in diesel and electrical engineering, have all been turned to good use. And several of the next generation, now in their teens, are already expressing the intention of making Fair Isle their permanent home.

Over the last 100 years the social scene has had its ups and downs, but the last three decades have seen a progressive increase in opportunities for introducing 'new blood', both through marriage with non-islanders and through the establishment of incoming settlers. In 1891 all but 16 of the 179 permanent residents were Fair Isle born, and the remainder were Shetlanders. Between 1785 and 1845 the number of surnames had dropped from 14 to eight, and by 1955 only four were represented among the crofters: Anderson, Eunson, Wilson and Stout. It was this predominance of only a few names that was responsible for the practice of referring to people by Christian and croft names, to overcome the chance of confusion as to which Jimmy or Jerry Stout, for example, was involved. Now, in the 1980s, less than half of the crofting community were born on the isle, or to parents then resident on the isle, and the others include people from as far away as the south of England. The number of surnames has risen again to ten, and there is a much better scatter of age groups than there was 30 years ago. Although the

Every stack and headland has a name. The spectacular rock finger in the foreground is The Sheriff.

Between trips 'Good Shepherd IV' sits snugly in her Buness 'noost' - a much more sheltered spot than the old slipway across the isle's one sandy beach.

From the old barn and kiln below Shirva the road winds down past Leogh and Melville House to the lighthouse standing sentinel at Skadan.

The style and siting typical of the 1890s improvement period can still be distinguished in many of the island's houses; Stackhoull Stores (left front) is of similar design.

Mechanisation has taken much of the drudgery out of crofting tasks - but many hands are still needed to make light work of haymaking.

Summertime - the 'Good Shepherd' and visiting yachts nestle at the North Haven pier.

After a gap of some 30 years, the craft of boatbuilding has recently been revived and still employs the broad, shallow design traditional for hundreds of years.

Experienced hand-knitters can work at a remarkable speed, resting the end of one needle in a belt-pad.

Fair Isle knitwear has long been famous for its wide variety of colours and patterns.

One corner of the museum represents a fireside scene typical of the past, with handmade straw-backed chair, woodlined walls and open peat fire.

The chance of seeing migrants like this handsome long-eared owl 'in the hand'
attracts many birdwatchers to the isle.

Throngs of endearingly comical puffins socialise on the grassy clifftops during the breeding season.

Thrift is among the colourful flowers which brighten the cliffs and meadows in spring and summer.

Pounding seas have carved an endless variety of shapes around Fair Isle's coastline; this arch is in South Harbour.

Whitewashed necklaces of Kittiwake nests and tiers of breeding Guillemots stand out against the sombre grey and deep red of the cliffs.

population is still small it is now looking ahead with hope rather than despair. The islanders enjoy a higher standard of living and are more prosperous than they have ever been in the past . . . but they can achieve this only by tackling a range of occupations, since no single job brings in sufficient income to maintain a family.

CHAPTER SEVEN

Making Ends Meet

Making a living has never been easy on Fair Isle. In the days when the island was truly isolated its inhabitants had to make the best possible use of the limited resources available to them, both those occurring naturally and those cast up by the sea, while nothing produced on the crofts was ever wasted. As shipping traffic increased on adjacent sea-routes the people added bartering and smuggling to their basic occupations of fishing and crofting. And as developments on the island itself opened up new opportunities for paid employment they turned their hands to such tasks as lighthouse relief work, road-making, and building construction. Over the years the range of activities undertaken in order to supplement a family's main source of income has gradually changed, but for at least four centuries production of the woollen goods for which the name Fair Isle is now famous has continued without a break.

The most obvious of Fair Isle's natural resources is its vast population of seabirds, which provided a valuable source of food in days gone by. According to a writer in 1769 the islanders' food consisted chiefly of milk, fish and the eggs and flesh of 'wild fowl which they procure among the precipices'. There were no fulmars present in those days but guillemots were caught with horse-hair snares, fixed to floating boards and known as 'paantrips', and no doubt puffins were taken from their burrows. Small land birds, such as snow buntings, were also snared, and rock doves were caught in their roosting caves by hanging a blanket over the cave mouth and then using a light to dazzle the birds and make them panic. In the 17th century the 'great multitude of sea fowls' were said also to be 'not a little beneficial to the islanders by reason of their feathers, which is a chief commodity of the place', and as late as 1804 about 6 stone of feathers were still being collected yearly, for sale to the proprietor at 3/— per stone. The risks run by the fowlers were considerable as 'they sometimes catch a slip whereby they are either crushed on the rocks or

For centuries the community was heavily dependent upon the island's natural resources. Eggs, 'fowls' and feathers were valuable sources of food and income until the end of last century.

drowned in the sea' and the practice was finally abandoned early this century.

While fowling might endanger the lives of the islefolk themselves, turf cutting presented a threat to the fertility of their crofting ground. Nowadays the old feelie dykes are the only surviving evidence that turf was once important as a building material, for the walls of houses and sheds as well as for roofing purposes. Most house roofs continued to be thatched with 'feels' covered with a thin layer of straw until early this century, and at least one turf-roofed shed was still in existence in 1962. Such a perishable roofing material required frequent renewal, which meant that grassy divots were constantly being skinned off the land surface, starving the soil beneath. When Fotheringhame carried out his inspection he found that the south end of the isle had been 'cut up in a most shameful manner'; as a result of his comments the lease drawn up for a new tacksman stipulated that 'he shall not cut nor shall he allow any of the Tenants or Inhabitants to cut upon any pretence whatever any part of the Turf or surface of the ground to the Southward of the Hill Dyke'.

Apart from turf and stone, which was laborious to work and heavy to move, the only available building material was driftwood cast up by the sea. Not surprisingly, such bounty was highly valued and much time was spent scouring 'da banks' and carrying any timber found safely above the high tide line. Whitewood planks — often carried as deck cargo and so liable to be swept overboard — were good for panelling work and furniture construction, roundwood logs were handy for roofing timbers, and wrecks often produced ready-made doors, complete with fittings. Molly Wilson, writing in 1963, recorded that all the furniture in Springfield, where she spent most of her life, had been made by her father or grandfather. Chairs, beds, dresser, girnals and kists (chests for storing meal and other dry goods, respectively) all originated as flotsam, while the doors leading out of the living-room came from the sailing ship *Black Watch*, wrecked off Skadan in 1877. Roof-beams for Upper Stoneybreck and a chain for use on Sheep Craig also came from that wreck.

'Beachcombing here is a hereditary passion, and of all his property the Fair Islander seems to treasure most the hoard of jetsam abaft his croft', wrote R. M. Lockley in the 1930s. And even today, when furniture is more often imported than island-made, the habit of 'saving' timber dies hard — and is by no means confined to those who inherited the practice. When the *Maverick* broke up in 1980 the daughter of a fairly recent settler wrote 'Dad got some fish-boxes and some plastic baskets' but, sadly, 'the big storm took Daddy's white wood away back into the sea'.

After a wreck the sea was likely to bring in other useful things besides wood. Rice is said to have come ashore from the *Lessing*, and flour — a welcome change from home-ground meal — from the *Canadia*, wrecked in 1915. And no doubt casks of spirits were retrieved more often than is recorded. One of the few documented cases was in 1816 when 52 ankers of gin were saved from the *Joanna en Pietrenella*, only to be seized by the customs! And in 1888 the finders of a small cask of brandy washed up in the North Haven dutifully handed it over to the authorities and received £1.6s as salvage reward.

Bartering was an important part of the Fair Isle way of life for at least 200 years. One of the earliest accounts dates from 1711, when a sailing ship returning from a round-the-world voyage, and incidentally bringing Alexander Selkirk (Robinson Crusoe) home, was becalmed off the isle and a yole went out to her with vegetables and other goods. And in 1774 poultry, eggs, dried fish and woollen goods were also on offer. In exchange for their produce the islanders might receive salt pork, bread, tobacco or spirits, and in later years books, sea-boots, dungarees and odd lengths of rope or canvas.

Not all skippers were willing to heave-to while bartering went on, so the islanders became adept at boarding a moving vessel — a risky business because their narrow yoles were liable to tip nose-down as the tow-line took the strain. When the ship being visited was some distance out there was also a risk that the weather might change while the yoles were still far from home. A sudden gale or fog could result in a disaster such as that of 1897 (referred to in Chapter 2) or in an unplanned sea voyage. In 1788, for example, fog came down suddenly while a boat was bartering three miles off shore. After five hours rowing, as they thought towards the isle, the crew found themselves back alongside the sailing ship and were taken aboard in an exhausted state. They awoke next morning to find the ship running before a westerly gale, her sails in ribbons. When she reached Elsinore in Denmark four days later the Fair Islanders were put ashore, but their return journey via Leith and Lerwick took 11 months — and they eventually arrived home to find the community mourning for them.

Opportunities for smuggling, as a sideline to straight bartering, were considerable, and the islanders made the most of them during the 18th and 19th centuries, often storing contraband spirits and tobacco in the 'Tiefs' Holes' below Malcolm's Head until they could be smuggled out to Shetland or Orkney. One tacksman's lease stipulated that he must not be concerned in illicit trade, nor allow the island to be 'either a resort for smugglers or a receptacle for contraband goods', but despite such decrees the practice apparently continued unabated, as the gin episode in 1816 involved his successor, James Strong, and a few years later an inspector of the Scottish Society for the Propagation of Christian Knowledge described the islanders as 'all professional smugglers'. The penalties for those caught were severe, as a traveller reported in 1832 after encountering three brothers who had arrived in Orkney with a few pounds of tobacco to trade for meal. When caught with the illicit goods they were taken into custody, for a possible prison sentence of several weeks, and their boat was seized. Such a punishment could be serious, as without a boat the men would be unable to provide for their families, either by smuggling or by legitimate means such as fishing and bartering. The 1863 edition of Chambers Journal said of Fair Isle 'A more convenient smuggling station there cannot be' but not long after that the trade started to dwindle and it was virtually abandoned by the end of the century, when opportunities for earning money, as opposed to receiving payment in kind, started to increase and the islanders tackled a variety of new tasks.

In the mid 1800s, with a still-growing population and limited resources on the island, some men had to seek seasonal employment elsewhere, often spending long periods away on a whaler or fishing boat. The census

Straw was an important commodity, not just for feeding to stock but also for making into chair-backs, baskets of various shapes and sizes, and ropes. Here it is being twisted into 'simmens' or ropes, probably for use in anchoring thatch (see p. 55).

records show that in 1861 five men were temporarily absent, four at the Greenland whale and seal fishing and one cod fishing in Faroe. Island jobs listed at that time included woollen weaver, fish curer, joiner, and boat carpenter (employing four labourers); among the womenfolk there was a spinner, a worsted knitter, a dressmaker and two midwives. Labouring jobs became available soon after that, with Bruce's road-making and building activities, and construction work on the lighthouses and piers. For brief spells in 1874, and again in 1917, there were also labouring jobs with the mining teams working at Copper Geo in North Naaversgill; the pay offered in 1917 was about 5/— for 10 hours work. By the end of the century part-time lighthouse relief had become a valuable source of income for several islanders, while coastguard duties and the Post Office provided employment for others. By then, too, some young women were spending a period in domestic service before settling down to married life; two who took jobs in Edinburgh after participating in the Exhibition of 1886 were possibly the first to go 'into service'. But there were still not nearly enough part-time jobs available on the island — and only part-time work can be fitted around the seasonal demands of fishing and crofting.

Employment opportunities improved during both world wars, when those not on active service had the chance of jobs such as camp construction and guarding the submarine telephone cable at the North Haven, and there was also a big increase in coastguard and other look-out duties. But after the 1939-45 war only sporadic paid employment was available for most of the men, on such tasks as road-repairing, ferrying goods by lorry from pier to lighthouses, and doing maintenance jobs associated with the telephone repeater station. Some people managed to line up an impressive list of ancillary occupations; in the 1950s Jerry Stout of Utra (Melville House) was Justice of the Peace, deputy Receiver of Wrecks, telephone linesman, operator of the GPO generators, Registrar of Births, Marriages and Deaths, island historian (unpaid) and general messenger (in the only van on the isle, which belonged to the GPO!), but not all were so fortunate. In order to support the rising standard of living by then expected, new sources of income were needed — and it was towards meeting this need that first George Waterston and then the National Trust for Scotland directed their attention.

In addition to developing the Bird Observatory, with its spin-off increase in freight and passenger income, trade on the isle, and caretaking-maintenance-domestic jobs, George had hopes of revitalising the fishing industry and expanding the knitwear trade. The lack of a safe harbour still limits potential as regards fishing, but his ideas for woollen goods

When copper was mined at North Naaversgill in 1917 an aerial ropeway was proposed for transporting it to the North Haven. But the location made mining dangerous and it was soon abandoned, bringing to an end the associated labouring jobs available to islanders.

were more realistic and the islanders' success in developing this craft is described later. Once the isle had passed into National Trust ownership jobs became available on projects aimed at improving living conditions, often with the islanders working alongside International Voluntary Service groups or other visiting parties of volunteers; the arrival in 1963 of a concrete mixer, stone-crusher and block-making machine greatly facilitated the modernisation of croft houses and steadings. In 1975 a local construction company, Northmen Ltd, was set up by two islanders, one of them a trained joiner; this partnership now contracts, or sub-contracts, for many of the building jobs, including the first sheltered housing on the isle, and employs others on a part-time basis.

Meanwhile other bodies were also undertaking projects and nearly all of these too resulted in employment of some sort both during construction and afterwards. In 1974 management of the generator electricity supply became the responsibility of the Fair Isle Electricity Council; an electrical engineer married to an island girl now also looks after the aerogenerator, which was the first commercially-operated windpower supply in Britain. And in 1978 a 'mains' water supply system was completed, and is maintained by one Water Board Representative. Other part-time jobs include meteorological reporting, cooking/cleaning/teaching at the school, maintenance work/relief cooking at the Bird Observatory, running Post Office and shop, operating the *Good Shepherd*, managing the airfield, running a haulage business (taxi/lorry/car hire), relief nursing, providing bed and breakfast, and the long-established duties of coastguard watch and — until the South Light too goes automatic — lighthouse relief. These many and varied opportunities for earning a little extra have all helped to make life more comfortable than it would otherwise be. But the ancillary occupation which has made the largest contribution to the islanders' income over by far the longest period is undoubtedly the production of the famous Fair Isle woollen goods.

Evidence of both knitting and hand-weaving in Norse times has reputedly been found in Shetland, and in all probability they date from the same period on Fair Isle. At the time of the Armada the islanders were certainly using sheep's wool as their principal clothing material; in 1769 James Robertson recorded that the women were continually employed in knitting stockings or gloves and spinning woollen yarn; and by 1774 the islanders were bartering 'knit caps, mittens, stockings and the softest coarse cloth I ever saw made of wool', as well as weaving cloth to make garments for their own use. Tradition has it that the characteristic Fair Isle patterns were learned from the Spaniards shipwrecked in 1588, but many of the designs are similar to those used in such widely scattered countries as Scandinavia, Bulgaria, Arabia and Egypt. Possibly the inspiration for some came from each source — and perhaps others originated on the island itself and symbolised different aspects of local life; it is unlikely that their true origins will ever be known for certain. Some 120 different patterns, many of which are identified by names, are displayed, as long scarves, in the island museum.

The first written reference to patterned knitwear seems to be an advertisement in the 'Shetland Advertiser' of January 1862, which read:

'FAIR ISLE HOSIERY. James R. Spence, 85 Commercial Street, has on hand a varied assortment of curiously Knitted Goods from the Fair Isle.'

Sales were probably stimulated by the 'Handbook to the Zetland Islands' published in 1867, which stated that 'Their hosiery is of a very peculiar appearance, the patterns and colours being of all descriptions and shades, while the softness and fineness of the wool . . . make it particularly popular as an article of clothing . . .', and a few years later Lerwick shop windows were said to be crowded with specimens of Fair Isle industry. A wider potential market was reached for the first time in 1886 when the Sheriff of Zetland arranged, with the help of William Laurence, for monthly relays of Fair Isle knitters to attend an International Exhibition in Edinburgh. Among the items displayed there were specimens of Fair Isle work presented to the Duke of Connaught (3rd son of Queen Victoria) on the occasion of his marriage in 1879 'in recognition of the valuable service he rendered in forwarding the arrangements for postal communication with the island'. Perhaps as a result of this publicity 'Those who are interested in the inhabitants of Fair Isle' were by 1897 being urged to 'do something to increase their comfort, and at the same time secure useful and beautiful articles of hosiery, by sending orders for knitted work to the island'. By that date, thanks to the efforts and financial backing of Sheriff Thoms, a Money-Order Office had been established on the isle, making 'cash' transactions easier than ever before.

According to the Official Guide to the 1886 Exhibition 'The hosiery from Fair Isle is of a very distinctive type, and may be known by its bright and varied colours with chequered patterns', and another late 19th century publication described it as 'quite a different sort . . . from that done in Shetland; . . . in patterns and colours dyed by the people themselves'. Until well into this century most of the colours used in the genuine Fair Isle knitwear came from vegetable dyes, generally made from the roots, stems and blooms of flowering plants. These vegetable dyes produced softer colours than chemical dyes and were surprisingly fast; even against a white background strong colours such as deep red did not run when washed. Knitwear made of undyed wool, in all the natural shades of moorit and grey/black, became increasingly popular around the middle of this century, and is still much in demand.

In the early 1920s Fair Isle patterns were given a welcome boost by the Prince of Wales, who wore a Shetland-made sweater when driving from the first tee at St Andrews as Captain of the (now Royal and) Ancient Golf Club. As these Shetland-made imitations proliferated, the need for

Fair Isle pattern knitwear was first publicised more than 100 years ago, and the islanders were bartering knitted goods long before that. Hand-knitters traditionally use four needles, and each employs her own characteristic combinations of patterns and colours. Straw-backed chairs like this, with two drawers for holding wool, were on offer at 30/– in 1898.

a trade mark to distinguish island-made goods became acute, and in 1924 Jerome Stout, the postmaster, travelled to London to present the Fair Isle knitters' case to the Board of Trade. Although he failed in his attempt to secure a unique mark for the island's goods, it was agreed that the Shetland trade mark should be over-printed with the words 'made in Fair Isle'. Home-dyeing was at that time a requirement for goods so marked, although chemical dyes had by then largely replaced the natural ones.

Traditional Fair Isle pattern knitwear involved the use of only two colours in any one row and was produced on four needles, which meant that the knitter could always see the right side of the work. With one needle resting in a straw-filled leather pad at the waist, work progressed at an astonishing speed. Because of their many other duties, however, the island women could devote only a proportion of their time to knitting and by the early 1960s the few remaining hand knitters were unable to satisfy demand. By then knitting machines had appeared on the isle, to be used initially for self-colour jumpers, to which patterned yokes were added. Such produce was not, of course, eligible for the 'Hand-made in Fair Isle' trademark, and consequently could not command top prices.

As knitwear production is a home industry which can be undertaken by men as well as women, and can be carried out as and when other tasks permit, it is particularly well suited to the Fair Isle situation — but to achieve its full earning potential maximum productivity and pricing are necessary. With this in mind, attention was directed towards mastering the art of producing all-over patterned goods on punch-card machines and to exploring the feasibility of establishing a knitting co-operative. When Fair Isle Crafts Ltd, was launched in 1980 it involved eight knitters, two finishers and a packer/administrator. A 'Good Housekeeping' article featuring a Fair Isle Crafts jumper brought in a lot of orders, and when the 'new style' goods were displayed at the Aviemore Craft Fair they attracted favourable comment. But the lack of a unique trademark limited the marketing opportunities — and this time application had to be made to the European Economic Community. The first design submitted was too similar to an established Swiss one, and it took several years of effort before the 'hand frame knitted' trademark was eventually registered.

Now, some nine years after it started, the craftwork co-operative provides part-time employment for 13 men and women, and its order books are full. Each week in summer a range of knitwear is displayed in the Community Hall, where visitors can either purchase goods or order the colours, styles and sizes they want. As in the past, every garment is

Since the 1870s coastguard duties and lighthouse relief work have provided regular part-time employment for several islanders, though this has decreased in recent years. A helicopter rescue service has now replaced the rocket lines and breeches buoy — and deprived adventurous youngsters of an exciting trip during practice sessions.

unique and each knitter uses his or her own individual choice of colours and designs.

As well as an increase in knitting activity, the period since the mid-1950s has also seen a revival of weaving, which had gradually declined since the turn of the century and ceased altogether in the 1930s. Weaving was one of the possibilities that George Waterston had identified as a potential source of income and when Zetland County Council offered to provide looms and an instructor for a trial 3 months six of the younger men applied for training. A Shetland weaver arrived in 1957 to give instruction on looms set up in the Bird Observatory's Coronation Hut — and subsequently spent five years at the Haa, with his family, as a crofter/weaver. By 1958 tweed, scarves and rugs were being produced in considerable quantities and were snapped up, like the knitwear, by visitors to the Observatory or those coming ashore from the National

Trust's *Meteor* and *Regina Maris* cruises. In 1961 the entire winter output of woollen goods was sold to cruise passengers.

Since travel to and from the North Haven wasted a considerable amount of time, it was planned to move the looms to the re-roofed fish store at Kirkigeo; but this plan was never implemented, partly because the site was not very convenient and partly because two of the weavers had left the isle. Instead the Barkland barn became a weaving shed; about 100 yards of tweed were produced there in the winter of 1970-71, but thereafter weaving again declined.

Spinning, too, has recently seen a revival on the island. At one time a regular activity in every household, it had died out early this century, probably because knitting was a more profitable use of time. Much of the island's wool was then sent to mills at Brora to be spun but, while certainly of Shetland origin, there was no guarantee that the wool which came back would be from Fair Isle fleeces. Since the late 1970s there has been renewed interest in spinning and, although most yarn is now spun and dyed in Shetland, several of the younger women card and spin fleeces of the natural colours they want to use for hand-knitting. Knitwear which is both hand-spun and hand-knitted by islanders can command an even higher price than other island-made goods.

Fair Isle has come a long way since its community depended for the essentials of everyday life on the island's natural resources, 'gifts' of the sea, and the products of crofting, but it is good that some of the old crafts still survive. Although sheep and cattle hides are no longer needed to make outer garments and the thonged 'rivlins' in regular use as footwear 100 years ago, sheepskins are still cured, for sale as rugs. The skills of spinning and weaving are still practised, albeit on a limited scale, and Fair Isle knitwear is still something special, even if it is produced on a machine. Most of the craft goods produced today are sold direct to visitors, so there is no need to involve a middle-man with consequent reduction in profit. But how different might the story of the island have been if visitors had not started to come to it by choice, rather than only by accident or in the course of duty?

CHAPTER EIGHT

Visitors Various

Many of Fair Isle's earliest visitors came either by chance, when passing en route to somewhere else or as a result of shipwreck, and today some still arrive for these reasons. Later came those whose visits were in the line of duty — for example factors, fish merchants and ministers coming to catechise their parishioners. Since early this century, however, most have come because they wanted to, and the range of visitors has widened progressively as transport services, landing facilities and accommodation improved. To all, whether shipwrecked mariner, 'ordinary' holiday-maker or important personage, the islanders extend the same warm welcome, and all — though admittedly in varying degrees — add something to the story of Fair Isle.

One of the earliest descriptions of the isle was recorded in the log of the *Gabriel*, during Martin Frobisher's first voyage in search of the north-west passage. On 24th June 1576 the *Gabriel's* Master wrote 'I had sight of Fair yle . . . it did rise at the Southernmost ende with a little hommocke, and swampe in the middes . . . I sailed to that Island to see whether there were any roadesteede for a Northwest winde, and I found by my sounding hard rockes, and foule ground, and deepe water, within two cables of the shoare . . . and so did not ancre under the Island.' Not long afterwards the first account of life on the island was written by the Spaniard whose diary of the Armada and the wreck of *El Gran Grifon* provides such a valuable record of those times.

The island's birds attracted attention in 1664, when Robert Marr (writing about Orkney) commented 'There are also many hawks; but the best is that of the fair Isle lying 30 miles from Orkney, and as far from Zetland, so that his flight is that long'. This statement, like many of the early descriptions, was subsequently much quoted by other writers, among them Martin Martin, Gent, of St Kilda fame, who mentions the Fair Isle hawks at the end of his 'A Description of the Western Isles of

The physical condition of these Spaniards was undoubtedly very different from that of the fellow countrymen they came to commemorate! After erecting a memorial in the cemetery, the party visited Stroms Heelor, where *El Gran Grifon* was wrecked in 1588. Beyond, the light is shining right through the caves under Sheep Craig.

Scotland'. Rev. James Kay expanded the account slightly, referring to 'an excellent Falcon, which nestles and hatches in this place, whose young ones are taken with the same difficulty and hazard that ye Sea Fowls before spoken of', and a few years later Rev. James Brand claimed that the Fair Isle hawks 'are the best in Britain' and that 'sometimes they'll find Moor Fowls in their Nests, which they behoved to bring from Orkney, seeing there are none in Zetland, and the nearest Isle they could have them in was Stronza, or Westra, which is between 40 and 50 Miles of sea over which at one flight they must carry these Fowls to their Nests'. It seems a long way to go for prey when there were abundant seabirds available on the spot.

Travellers passing by in the 18th century included Captain Woodes Rogers, a navigator and explorer who made a round-the-world trip in the course of which he rescued Alexander Selkirk from the uninhabited island of Juan Fernandez — and provided inspiration for Defoe's

Robinson Crusoe. In July 1711, when Rogers was nearing 'the Conclusion of a fatiguing voyage' — it had lasted more than three years — his ship lay off Fair Isle while 'Boats came to and fro all Night, and supply'd us with what we wanted.' James Robertson, touring Orkney and Shetland in 1769, actually spent about four days on the isle — not intentionally but because a contrary wind obliged him to land there. He took this opportunity of 'scanning' the island and, in addition to describing its physical features, reported that 'the people speak English with a considerable degree of the Norse accent. They are very hospitable to strangers and live in the utmost peace and harmony with each other'. Miss J. Schaw, whose narrative of a journey from Scotland to the West Indies in 1774 was published under the delightful title 'Journal of a Lady of Quality', did not go ashore but clearly paid close attention to the occupants of the boats which came off to barter. 'They are of middling stature, strong built and straight, their complexions uncommonly fair, their skins remarkably smooth, their features high, aquiline noses and small eyes. Their hair is not red but real yellow and the older ones wore it long on the bottom of their chins which are very peaked. They wore red caps lined with skin and Jackets of the same with a Paulice (pelisse) of coarse cloth and boots of undressed skin, with the rough side outmost, over which were trousers made of cloth.'

Two famous writers, Sir Walter Scott and Robert Louis Stevenson, and at least one artist were among those who visited in the nineteenth century. In August 1814 Scott, visiting Shetland with the Commissioners of Northern Lights, came ashore for a single day — at the second attempt, as the tide had carried the lighthouse yacht far to the east on the northbound trip. Sir Walter expressed the view that 'an equal space of rich land on Fair Isle, situated in an inland county of Scotland, would rent for £3000 at the very least'. Perhaps he was simply quoting James Strong, the tacksman at that time, with whom he dined in the Haa; considerately, or perhaps wisely, he had the meal sent ashore from the yacht 'so as not to overburthen his hospitality'. According to Scott, teacher John Irvine (the one who claimed to catechise 108 young people every Sunday) was a drunkard, while the islanders greatly regretted the American war and the happy days when they could get a bottle of peach brandy or rum in exchange for a pair of worsted stockings or a dozen eggs.

Robert Louis Stevenson's visit in June 1869, when accompanying his father on the Northern Lighthouse Board steamer *Pharos*, was equally brief and produced equally pithy comments. He described the island as an 'unhomely, rugged turret-top of submarine sierras' and its population as 'sore-eyed, short-living, inbred fishers'. Not surprisingly, in view of the lapse of time, he found the islanders very unwilling to talk about the

During World War II the few Shetland ponies still kept on the isle again became beasts of burden, carrying supplies up to the gun site near the summit of Ward Hill. Until the late 19th century all goods were transported on the backs of either ponies or people.

Armada wreck, but he nevertheless unearthed a legend that the shipwrecked men, when standing hand in hand, reached right across the island — the mind boggles at the idea of them actually doing this!

The first artist known to have visited Fair Isle arrived in 1868, a few weeks after the *Lessing* had been wrecked. He was John Reid, whose book 'Art Rambles in Shetland' includes a lithograph of the wreck and an account of the rescue. While both must have depended to some extent on imagination, his claim that 'gloomy pictures of famine filled the troubled minds' of the island women, when they saw the number of survivors coming ashore, seems likely to be valid. Like many another early visitor, Reid had difficulty reaching the isle; fog forced the first attempt to be abandoned, and on the second a strong tide was running off the north end, so that 'we beat about for more than three hours without gaining an inch'.

By the end of the 19th century it was a bit easier to get there; a special trip by the *Earl of Zetland* was advertised in 1886 as affording 'an excellent opportunity to anyone desirous of paying a visit to that lonely isle to do so at a cheap rate'. And from the early 1900s the occasional wealthy yachtsman was calling in, among them the philanthropist James Coats, Junior, of Paisley. His chance visit resulted not only in treatment for a sick child and sales of all available knitwear, but also medical supplies and Christmas parcels for many years, and gifts ranging from sewing machines and a pianola to 300 tins of cocoa! It was not until 1905, however, that anyone from outwith the Northern Isles set out with the specific intention of making more than a brief, casual visit to the island.

Among the earliest to do so was Dr William Eagle Clarke, the first person fully to appreciate Fair Isle's value as an observation point for bird migration. Although a list of Fair Isle's birds appeared in Evans and Buckley's 'Vertebrate Fauna of the Shetlands' (1897), it was not based on first-hand knowledge as the authors did not visit the island, of which they commented 'there is so little information obtainable as regards the Fauna'. The list they presented had been compiled in 1881 by the indefatigable William Laurence, teacher and man of many parts, and contained a mere 49 'species' (the identity of some, eg 'Sheldrake, Small.' can only be guessed at); it included 'Skua Gull, Turtle Dove here occasionally' and, surprisingly, titmice. Laurence's total was to be more than quadrupled within 30 years.

Eagle Clarke's first visit took place in 1905. A museum curator by profession, he was appointed to a British Association committee set up to investigate the migration of birds in the British Isles, and embarked on a series of study visits to islands and lighthouses in order to obtain first-hand experience of bird movements. Looking for a site which might be comparable to Heligoland, already known for its regular passage of migrants, Eagle Clarke selected Fair Isle because: it appeared to lie right in the flight line of hosts of migrants; it was isolated and therefore likely to be a welcome resting-place for migrants; and its moderate size meant that it should be possible 'to ascertain, with some degree of accuracy, what species were present daily'. Although the last turned out to be more difficult than he had anticipated, his prediction that the isle would prove important was more than realised, and his book 'Studies in Bird Migration' (1912) established Fair Isle as 'the most famous bird observatory in our islands'.

Between 1905 and 1911 Eagle Clarke came eight times, in spring and autumn, and by the end of this period he and his companions had recorded no fewer than 207 species, about half the number known ever to have occurred in the British Isles. During his initial visit he had

Holidaymakers aboard cruise ships often enjoy unusual and impressive views of the isle, in this case the 'iron precipice' of Sheep Craig's south face. Not all such travellers manage to come ashore, but many see enough to draw them back for a proper visit.

discovered that 16 year old George Stout of Busta was already knowledgeable about the island's birds. Given identification books, field glasses and a few weeks' training George soon demonstrated that he was a reliable observer and was appointed 'official recorder', responsible for making observations when no visiting ornithologist was on the island.

Others who helped Clarke with this work included Norman Kinnear, later to become Director of the British Museum of Natural History, and the Duchess of Bedford — who came in her private yacht *Sapphire*, as well as George Stout's brother Stewart and cousin Jerome Wilson of Springfield.

'Studies in Bird Migration' includes several statements which highlight both differences and similarities between bird study then and now. 'In time one becomes more or less familiar with most species, and readily detects a stranger — but only as a stranger until it has been brought to hand: one must shoot in such cases; if not, the identity of some of the visitors would remain a mystery'. Today, thankfully, trapping has replaced shooting, but otherwise the situation remains the same. 'The occurrences of rare birds have always had a peculiar charm for ornithologists' and still do, although in the case of some 'twitchers' it seems to become a craze rather than a charm! It is also still true that 'Only species with a predilection for open country' are in evidence after a fall of migrants, 'the rest skulking on croft ground'. The book includes some charming descriptions: of woodcock on the grassy ledges of the west cliffs 'resting in their usual posture, with their tails up and their bills down'; of goldcrests 'creeping in numbers on the faces of the gaunt, lichen-spangled precipices'; and of a hawfinch digging its bill into pony dung and 'so engrossed in its occupation that it allowed a close approach'. Eagle Clarke's main purpose was, however, to present theories regarding the conditions governing migration, a topic which is covered in a later chapter.

After World War I Eagle Clarke visited Fair Isle again, this time with Surgeon Rear-Admiral John H. Stenhouse, who was to continue bird studies on the island until 1928. The flow of notes on 'new' species also resumed, mostly published in the 'Scottish Naturalist' and written by Clarke, Stenhouse, Jerome Wilson and the second George Stout, of Field, affectionately known by all his friends as 'Fieldy'. These, and reports of the amazing range of migrants to be seen on Fair Isle, attracted other birdwatchers enthusiastic enough to tackle the considerable difficulty and inconvenience of getting to, and finding accommodation on, the island. Among these enthusiasts was the young George Waterston — of whom more in the next chapter.

From 1939 to 1945 the isle had few visitors other than those involved in erecting, occupying and supplying the naval camp at the North Haven and the army billets at Pund (which was burnt out during this period) and the Haa. In addition to losing several men on active service, Fair Isle was directly affected by the war in other ways. Mines were washed in on a number of occasions; one exploded near Kirkigeo, blowing out windows at Melville House and dislodging the heavy slates on the roof, while

Life for Puffinn residents is not all work and no play; volunteer groups repay islanders' hospitality by organising barbecues and challenge the local football team. These social encounters can be as valuable a part of the visitors' stay as the work that they do.

Fieldy claimed to have sunk at least one with a rifle. Enemy aircraft dropped bombs on the South Lighthouse, killing the wife and daughter of the principal keeper, and a soldier died of wounds received from machine gun fire during the same attack. Most signs of wartime activities have now gone; the radar station and nearly all the other buildings on Ward Hill were demolished in 1961 but the remains of a Heinkel which crash-landed on Vaasetter in 1941 can still be seen. Three of the plane's crew survived and one, the pilot, revisited Fair Isle in 1987.

When the Bird Observatory eventually opened in 1948 the pre-war trickle of visitors became a steady stream, bringing ornithologists from all over the world. In its first short season of only eight weeks, the hostel catered for 16 birdwatchers, one of whom recorded the cost of his trip. With first class rail from London to Aberdeen, steamer fares, two nights in Henderson's Hotel at Spiggie, buses, taxis, the *Good Shepherd* and a week at the hostel his holiday cost him only £28.1.3d! By 1987 the Observatory had attracted people from no fewer than 26 countries out-

with the UK, including South Africa, Australia, New Zealand, Japan and
North America. So far there have been none from Russia, the Far East or
South America — but no doubt this deficiency will be remedied in due
course.

Fair Isle's acquisition by the National Trust for Scotland in 1954
brought wider publicity, and visitors continued to increase in both
numbers and variety. Annual visits by the *Earl of Zetland* from Lerwick,
and the *Orcadia* from Kirkwall, brought hundreds of day trippers in the
1950s, 1960s and 1970s, while the work camps run on the isle from 1962
onwards enabled volunteers from many different countries and walks of
life to spend a week or two helping with development projects and
experiencing the island way of life. And, weather permitting, passengers
on the annual National Trust cruise ships came ashore — and boosted
knitwear sales. Some 200 visitors were ferried ashore from the *Earl of
Zetland* and the *Meteor* for the opening ceremony for the new pier,
nearly quadrupling the island's population for the day. Fortunately that
occasion was blessed with glorious weather. Visits to the isle are now
included in some natural history package holidays to Shetland, and
parties occasionally charter a plane so that they can spend a few hours on
the isle.

That even a day visit can be a memorable occasion is well illustrated in
a poem by Sir John Betjeman, then Poet Laureate, who was on one of the
NTS cruises:

> 'To the people of Fair Isle we send salutation.
> Your arches and cliffs in the sun shining clear,
> From Skroo down to Scadden we made exploration,
> Each wonder we saw told us more would appear.
> And chiefly your kindness, Fair Isle, we remember,
> And sadly the *Meteor* sails from your shore.
> May the mists of July and the storms of December
> Preserve you, and keep you, to see us once more.'

As 'outside' interest in Fair Isle increased so too did attention from the
media. The first BBC visit was in 1954, to make recordings for 'In the
country', produced by Archie P. Lee; one of the stars of that programme
was Utra Jerry, with his comments that he had never married because he
had been too busy, and that if you slipped over the cliff it would not be
the fall that hurt you but the sudden stop. A BBC TV camera team
visited, with bird recordist Eric Simms, in 1963, to be followed by many
others: in 1970 helicopter shots of the isle featured in the 'Bird's Eye
View' programme; in 1984 Bill Oddie with the BBC, Diana Rigg with

When Her Majesty the Queen visited the isle in 1960 she travelled in a somewhat unusual 'royal carriage'! At that time there were not enough cars on the island to provide transport for the whole Royal party.

STV and a Norwegian crew were all filming — and the Observatory staff managed to 'borrow' the STV helicopter for a day to instal a new chain, presented by BP Shetland, on Sheep Craig; and in 1986 the RSPB film unit took shots of an albino puffin, the first recorded since Eagle Clarke saw one in 1908. Journalists and reporters from many areas have visited too — and subsequently published accounts ranging from factually correct to romantic rubbish.

Although the majority of visitors to the hostel (now known as the Lodge) have been interested primarily in natural history, and have included many other 'ists' besides ornithologists, Fair Isle has attracted those concerned with other studies too. In 1955 John Graham recorded folk tales for the Shetland Folklore Archive, and in 1962 Sandy Fenton, of the National Museum of Antiquities of Scotland, documented old crofting, fishing and domestic practices and equipment. Several wreck surveys, including the systematic exploration of *El Gran Grifon*, were carried out in the 1970s, and in 1983 a promising site discovered by one of the islanders was investigated by the Scottish Development Department's Ancient Monuments Division, leading in turn to Bradford

University's three-year archaeological survey. These varied studies, together with the natural history projects described in a later chapter, have contributed towards making Fair Isle one of the most fully documented of Scotland's islands.

There have also been an impressive number of VIP visitations, of which two stand out as particularly noteworthy. Perhaps of greatest significance was the gathering of officials and others who arrived in June 1956, aboard the Fisheries cruiser *Brenda*, to inspect the isle as a preliminary to discussing its future. At that time no fewer than seven of the 16 households were seriously thinking of leaving, so the island's future was very much in the balance. The 1956 Fair Isle Conference persuaded the islanders that action could and would be taken to improve conditions, and successfully tipped the scales towards a continuing community.

A highlight of a different kind was the Royal visit in August 1960. The *Britannia*, heading south from Lerwick, anchored off the South Harbour on the evening of the 11th and a party including Her Majesty the Queen, the Duke of Edinburgh, Princess Alexandra and Prince Michael came ashore by launch — to be greeted with a 21 gun salute (by shotguns!). Transport to Taft, for tea beside the open peat fire, and thence to the village hall, was on Leogh Jerry's lorry, specially spruced up for the occasion. At the hall the party saw hand-knitting demonstrations and accepted gifts of knitwear and weaving, and a celebratory beacon was lit on Ward Hill as the *Britannia* departed.

Increasing contact with visitors, from varied backgrounds and with equally varied interests, has effectively been widening the islanders' horizons since the early part of the present century. Those visitors who stayed long enough to make real contact with the isle folk were bringing new insights into what was happening in the world outside long before TV arrived, just as each change of teacher brought new ideas and methods into the school. But there has been only one individual visitor whose influence was to have a major and lasting effect on the island's economy — and that was George Waterston.

CHAPTER NINE

Fulfilment of a Dream

George Waterston was in his early twenties when he first came to Fair Isle. He had become a keen birdwatcher while still at school and was a frequent visitor to the Royal Scottish Museum, where he encountered J. H. Stenhouse and the 'good ladies' of Scottish ornithology, the Misses E. V. Baxter and L. J. Rintoul — all of whom were migration and island enthusiasts. Before long George 'caught the infection' and was following in their footsteps, visiting first Baxter and Rintoul's favourite haunt, the Isle of May, and then, in September 1935, Fair Isle.

On that first visit George and his friend Archie Bryson travelled on the *St Magnus* from Leith and were taken ashore by yole. They stayed with Nurse Munro and soon got to know Fieldy, with whom they scoured the island for migrants, armed with guns as well as binoculars. A walking-stick gun given to George by Admiral Stenhouse's widow was even taken to church. In the evenings they skinned the birds 'grassed' during the day; these included two fulmars asked for by the Royal Scottish Museum — which proved particularly difficult, and unpleasant, to deal with. On subsequent visits George usually stayed with Fieldy in his croft house, where furnishings were sparse and meals unpredictable, apart from consisting almost exclusively of mutton. He often recalled one memorable occasion when the main dish was sheep's head broth complete with hair and eyes!

George's dreams for Fair Isle began to take shape soon after his 1935 visit. Plans for a bird migration station came first, his aim being to establish an observatory similar to the one already in existence on the Isle of May. With Pat Venables, a keen ornithologist from England, he discussed the feasibility of constructing a Heligoland trap below the mills in Finniquoy (the Gully). At that time it was thought necessary to provide tree and shrub cover where a bird trap was to be sited; Pat was to send sycamore, rowan and elder plants and Theo Kay of Lerwick offered to provide rabbit netting. Before long the plan had expanded to include use of the cottage at Pund to accommodate birdwatchers, and George approached the British Trust for Ornithology for financial assistance. That request was turned down, as was a proposal put to the Scottish Ornithologists' Club that it should take on responsibility for both trap and cottage, but despite these discouragements the trees were duly planted and in autumn 1938 were reported to be surviving periodic salty sprays. That autumn also saw visits to Fair Isle by the eminent ornithologist H. F. Witherby, with P. A. D. Hollom and C. A. Norris — Fair Isle's fame as an observation point was clearly still spreading.

There is no surviving record of ornithological events on Fair Isle in the summer of 1939, but at the outbreak of World War II George, who was already a Territorial with the Royal Artillery, was immediately mobilised. He was serving in Crete when it fell to the Germans in 1941 and was eventually taken prisoner. While caged — and an article sent at the time to 'Bird Notes' shows that that is how he felt — in Offlag VIIB George occupied his mind in reading of others' island experiences, and in writing descriptive articles about Fair Isle and making plans — for the future of the island as a whole, as well as for a bird observatory. His plans involved either persuading the National Trust for Scotland to buy the island as a nature reserve or buying it himself, and recognised that the scheme's success would be dependent upon obtaining the whole-hearted co-operation and support of the island community — and upon introducing 'new blood' from Shetland. Ideas for the bird observatory included not only the construction of traps at both the Gully and the Haa, but also the alteration and extension of Pund, or Ortolan Cottage as it had been christened by the Duchess of Bedford, to accommodate a warden and his wife and 12 visitors. These proposals were complete with scale drawings, artist's impressions of the finished result, lists of furnishings, and estimates of capital required (£6,000) and profit expected. There were even notes on provisions to be ordered and sample menus — and a job specification for a 'maid servant'. She was to be a good, plain cook, to live out, and to work from 7.00am — 2.00pm and 6.00 — 9.00pm (no mention of a day off), for £1 per week plus meals!

In 1943 George, by then suffering badly from the kidney trouble which had first afflicted him as a schoolboy and was to dog the rest of his life, was repatriated, and rejoiced that his first sight of home was the familiar bulk of Sheep Craig. Surely this was a good omen for the future! The following March, between kidney operations, he returned to Fair Isle, cadging a lift from Orkney on a naval launch and staying at Shirva with the Nurse. During that visit he began to think of the Haa as a possible alternative to Pund, and made tentative plans to move some of

When the Bird Observatory was housed in the old naval hut visitors had to brave the weather as they moved between bedrooms, dining-room and commonroom, and on windy days the lino flapped on the floor. The 'Obs' trap between the huts caught some interesting birds over the years — and occasionally saved the washing from being blown out to sea.

the naval huts from the North Haven there to form an accommodation 'wing'. By the end of the year, however, the possibility of leaving the huts where they were and establishing the observatory at the North Haven had been suggested.

The next two years were frustrating in the extreme for George. Until mid-1945 he was still hoping to spend his summers on Fair Isle putting his various schemes into action, and to find winter employment in Edinburgh. Throughout that year he bombarded Theo Kay and several of the islanders with letters: trying to stir up support for an air ambulance service, encouraging the rehabilitation work at the Haa, and pressing towards acquisition of the naval huts and their contents. But permits were needed for nearly all materials and no project costing more than £10 could be started without one; even George was unable to sidestep the restrictions and red-tape, but some progress was nevertheless made. In late June 1945 Captain Fresson landed, with Basil Neven Spence MP, on the hill airstrip; a few days later George wrote to Theo 'I've got the dough to float the project'; and by late autumn the furniture from the naval huts had been handed over and stored at Pund. It was by then clear, however, that the opening of the observatory was still some way off, and no suitable part-time job had been found, so George reluctantly accepted that he would have to return to the family business.

For him the highlight of 1945 must surely have been his September visit to Fair Isle with Arthur Duncan and Ian Pitman, who were to play a major role in the affairs of the bird observatory for many years to come. He had got to know Arthur through their mutual involvement with the Scottish Ornithologists' Club, and had met Ian in POW camp; his enthusiastic presentation of the island's potential for migration studies had already captured their interest and this visit set the seal on their support for the venture. The weather was ideal — for enjoying the island if not for bringing in birds — with sun all week and a calm enough sea to permit a trip by yole up the east coast, passing through the Shaldi Cliff natural arch (site of the *Lessing* rescue) and the cave under Sheep Craig and climbing the Rock itself. Good food was provided for them by Hannah Stout at Rock Cottage, and they slept in reasonable comfort in an ex-army hut at Pund.

After his friends had left George stayed on for another three weeks, doing repairs at the Haa, working with the islanders on the construction of a trap in the garden there, assessing the potential of the huts and furnishings at the North Haven, and compiling a flora of Fair Isle with Hannah Stout. He even managed to ring a few birds, caught either in outhouses or at the lighthouse, before the trap was finally completed.

In 1946, although quite a lot of work had been done to the Haa it was

The opening of the new 'Lodge' in 1969 was a happy occasion for the three
whose efforts had been responsible not only for getting the Observatory started
but also for keeping it going during 21 often difficult years: (l. to r.) Ian Pitman,
Sir Arthur Duncan and George Waterston.

still not ready for occupation — but the North Haven huts were finally
vacated. On his September visit that year George was again accompanied
by Archie Bryson, together with Admiral Stenhouse's son Bruce and bird
artist Donald Watson. Between birding trips the four worked in the Haa
garden, digging, planting and repairing the trap. The sighting of a yellow-
breasted bunting marked an important turning point on the birdwatching
front: a serious discussion as to whether or not it was necessary to shoot
the bird in order to confirm this eighth record of the species in Britain. By
the time a decision had been reached, and the gun brought to the scene,
the bird had wisely departed!

At the beginning of 1947 the establishment of the bird observatory still
seemed nearly as far away as ever, but later in the year the situation
suddenly changed. The huts and their remaining contents passed into
George's possession and, better still, Fair Isle came on the market. By
early 1948 George was the island's owner, having purchased it from
Sumburgh Estate for £3,500, almost exactly the same price as John Bruce
had paid in 1866. That purchase became possible was largely thanks to
Ian Pitman, whose enthusiasm for the project persuaded Lord Bruntisfield
to offer an interest free loan. With the way clear at last, George threw

himself with renewed energy into the task of setting up and staffing his long-planned bird observatory.

By then he was married and back with the family business in Edinburgh, so it was necessary to find a director/warden to take charge of work on the island. Kenneth Williamson, an expert field ornithologist with museum training, arrived on Fair Isle in early June 1948. With the islanders' help he and his wife patched, plumbed and painted, laid lino, hung curtains, erected book-shelves and built traps. There were endless problems to be overcome during this post-war period of shortages. The Board of Trade refused permits for linen and furniture, and the second-hand blankets sent direct to the isle had to be returned south for cleaning as there was no laundry in Shetland. Some of the furniture brought in on the coal boat was infested with woodworm. And food supplies were poor, due not just to rationing but partly because the *Good Shepherd* was undergoing repairs and the isle was being supplied only fortnightly by the drifter *Lord Curzon*. Letters flowed fast (or as fast as they could!) and furious between Ken and George. Ken: we propose to salvage stoves from Ward Hill; please send a couple of thousand saccharins and half a dozen tins of coffee; dish towels needed urgently, and soap; please send 12 bottles salad-oil and fresh fruit, none available in Shetland; suggest you graze 20 ewes for hostel use on Skadan; half a Schoolton sheep booked for your September visit; I suggest we use an engine from Ward Hill to supply electricity for the hostel. George: Ian and I approve your plans; dish-cloths need ½ coupon each; soap substitute and tinned rhubarb sent, also a stuffed tawny owl to lure birds into traps.

When George visited briefly in late summer good progress had been made, despite all the problems, and the place was reckoned habitable. On 28th August the official opening was celebrated with a tea party, to which all the isle folk were invited. By the end of September traps were in operation at the Haa and the Gully, on Ward Hill (over a heap of war-time barbed wire) and along the Gilsetter dyke; Ken had designed the 'automatic' catching-box now widely used in bird traps; and 'lights on' at the hostel had been celebrated with a film show by Theo Kay. And on 1st October a public appeal for Fair Isle Bird Observatory Trust (FIBOT) was launched in Edinburgh and the funds necessary to run the operation began to come in. After four years of struggle the Observatory, keystone of George's scheme for the island, was at last a going concern.

During the 40 years since its formal opening the Observatory has had its ups and downs. The three key office-bearers elected when FIBOT was set up — chairman Arthur Duncan (later knighted for services to conservation), treasurer Ian Pitman, and secretary George Waterston — were to remain in those positions for more than 30 years, during which the Trust survived a number of financial crises. The modest £1.1s. per annum initially asked of 'Friends of Fair Isle' brought in a steady, though relatively small, income and the hostel operation seldom paid its way in the early years. Without generous grants from charitable trusts — notably the Pilgrim Trust, whose gifts not only met immediate needs but also allowed an Endowment Fund to be established, and the Dulverton Trust — and support from the National Trust for Scotland and the Nature Conservancy the Observatory would have been unable to survive.

The old war-time huts continued in use for more than 20 years, but eventually had to be replaced. Once again George launched a public appeal, this time for £10,000, to support the financial assistance offered by the Highlands and Islands Development Board. Thanks to grants from the National Trust for Scotland's Wildlife Fund, and the Pilgrim, Dulverton, and Carnegie Trusts, the necessary funds were raised and in autumn 1969 a new timber building, prefabricated in Devon and brought by sea from Berwick-on-Tweed, was ready to open, just eight weeks after the observatory's 21st birthday. In the presence of almost all the islanders and many other guests, the Earl of Wemyss, President of the National Trust for Scotland, declared the building open and recalled the vision and enterprise shown by George Waterston, Ian Pitman and Arthur Duncan in establishing the Observatory. For the first time since 1946 these three were together on the isle on this happy occasion, which included a 21st birthday cake, films and slides, and an evening of music, with the island band playing for songs and dancing.

George's active involvement in FIBOT affairs continued, despite his deteriorating health. Fortunately Irene, his second wife, shared his love of Fair Isle and its birds; with her support he was able to go on visiting the isle, sometimes accompanied by a portable kidney dialysis machine, until only months before he died. Many changes naturally took place in the running of the Observatory over the years — and George supervised virtually all of them. The Williamsons were succeeded in turn by Peter and Angela Davis, Roy and Marina Dennis, Roger and Judy Broad, Iain and Sally Robertson, and Nick and Liz Riddiford. From 1955 a steady flow of Assistant Wardens (of which the author of this book was the first, working like George's prospective maid for £1 a week plus keep!) helped with the ornithological work and benefited from the thorough training they received under the current Warden. And on the domestic side support staff changed from maids to cook-caterer plus assistant — but the informal atmosphere, with visitors giving a helping hand, remained a characteristic of the place. Needless to say the accommodation charge gradually crept up from the £5.5s a week (includes use of bicycles and bird rings) of the 1949 prospectus — but visitors no longer needed to

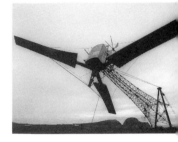

One of George's early ideas for improving life on Fair Isle was to harness the wind to produce electricity. In 1982 this dream became reality when the island's aero-generator was commissioned, establishing the first commercial wind-powered scheme in Britain.

bring their own soap, towel and ration book! Visitor numbers topped 400 visitor weeks for the first time in 1970, and more general-interest, as distinct from specifically 'birdy', people started coming to the Observatory. Growing numbers of young naturalists in the 15-20 age range benefited from the John Harrison Memorial Fund's help towards meeting the costs of a visit to Fair Isle, and party bookings for Young Ornithologists' Club members started to attract an even younger age group. All went well until well through the seventies, when once again external factors affected FIBOT.

When George made his last visit, only months before his death in September 1980, economic recession, escalating domestic travel costs, and ever-expanding opportunities for exciting birdwatching in many different parts of the world were having an adverse impact on visitor numbers and resulting in loss, rather than profit, on the hostel account. Although by then very ill, he nevertheless took a close interest in the programme of promotion, both at home and abroad, which helped to swing the pendulum the other way, and would have been delighted that numbers were starting to increase again by 1985. When this trend continued through 1986-87 the FIBOT Directors, though perhaps less unreservedly optimistic than George himself had been, were encouraged to look seriously, yet again, at the need for major building improvements.

Now more than 18 years old, the 'Lodge' was obviously suffering from the harsh climatic conditions to which buildings on Fair Isle are exposed, and expert advice suggested that the most practical remedy would be to encase it in harled blockwork. Early in 1988 — in the well-established Waterston tradition — a 40th Anniversary Appeal was launched. With the prospect this time of grant aid from the European Economic Community's Regional Development Fund, in addition to assistance from the various bodies which had helped in the past, plans were prepared and work started in late summer 1988. The rehabilitated building, with better kitchen facilities and self-catering accommodation for research workers, was ready for use by the start of the 1989 season. And with a predicted life of at least 40 more years it should ensure FIBOT's future well into the 21st century, a situation which, for all his vision and enthusiasm, George Waterston can hardly have anticipated when he was planning his observatory away back in 1941.

In addition to seeing his dreams for a bird observatory on Fair Isle fulfilled, George also had the satisfaction of seeing many of his other hopes for the island's development come to fruition. Although his ideas initially focused on bird study, he had soon realised that the future of the human community could not be considered secure until many aspects of life on the island had been brought into keeping with the times. The

George's plans for a museum also took a long time to reach fruition. The collection of crofting implements and household goods assembled in the early 1970s had to remain in temporary premises until the old village hall became available. These and many more items are now displayed in the George Waterston Memorial Centre.

development scheme he drew up while a prisoner of war included the statement that 'The primary idea underlying the entire scheme is the resuscitation of the economic life of the island. The island could be restored to a happy thriving community where the young people would feel assured of a definite future living on the island.' George anticipated the advent of air transport, and was confident that when it became available large numbers of birdwatching enthusiasts would be attracted to the isle, and would provide a useful, if limited, market for produce and hosiery. His scheme outlined proposals for the reintroduction of weaving, co-operative marketing of knitwear and other produce (with a protected trademark), the improvement of amenities, a progressive agricultural policy, the preservation of local traditions and crafts, the harnessing of wind-power for electricity, and even the construction of a breakwater in the North Haven.

But it soon became evident, even to the eternally-optimistic George, that boundless enthusiasm could not compensate for financial constraints, and that much outside help would be necessary in order to bring about the developments so urgently needed. In the earliest drafts of his scheme he had noted that acquisition of the isle by the National Trust for Scotland was one possible option, so it was natural that he should turn to the Trust for assistance once he had accepted that only 'public' ownership could offer real prospects of a secure future for the island. The transfer of ownership to the NTS took place in 1954, at a time when many of the younger islanders were becoming increasingly concerned about the problems of poor communications, lack of amenities, and limited social opportunities. Spurred on by talk of possible evacuation, the Trust and George — who acted as Trust factor for some years — together set about stimulating interest in the island's plight and support for any action that could be taken to alleviate it. One result of their efforts was the Fair Isle Conference of 1956, which brought together representatives of central and local government and a wide range of other agencies with the potential to contribute towards the island's well-being, and from that stemmed the support necessary for the implementation of many other aspects of George's scheme.

The provision of basic amenities, which was clearly of primary importance, proceeded apace from the late 1950s. Most of the houses had been modernised and provided with electricity and reliable piped water supplies by the mid 1970s; the new deep-water pier was completed in 1958; the air ambulance service started in 1967, charter flights in 1969 and a scheduled service in 1976. The going was not always easy, however, and not every islander welcomed and supported all these developments. Somewhat surprisingly — to an outsider — it was the introduction of a regular air service which caused most misgivings; there was very real concern that this might present a threat to the viability of the mailboat through loss of the Post Office contract. In the event the mail continued to be carried by the *Good Shepherd*, and probably no islander would now wish to see the air links with Shetland and Orkney withdrawn.

A few of George's early proposals were not entirely realistic — for example the production of Fair Isle cheese, re-damming of the Mill Burn to create a trout loch, and the marketing of gulls' eggs. And some of his proposed developments 'hung fire' for a long time, taking off only when the Fair Islanders themselves became convinced of their merits. One such was his vision of a craft co-operative, eventually realised a matter of months before his final visit to the isle, when he attended the official opening of the new Community Hall in June 1980. The renewed optimism of the community on that occasion must surely have gladdened his heart.

Since his death still more of George's ideas have been implemented, the most tangible of these being the introduction of wind-powered electricity and the establishment of the museum. The basis for the latter was laid back in 1972, when Gordon Barnes started to gather together in the Setter barn a collection of old crofting and fishing implements, household goods and other relics of bygone days. Over the years the Haa and Barkland were considered as possible museum sites, but it was only when the old village hall became redundant in 1980 that plans began to make progress, and it took several years to complete the necessary re-roofing and other improvements to the building and preparation of the exhibits. The formal opening of the museum, known as the George Waterston Memorial Centre, took place on 18th June 1986, when the ceremony was combined, happily, with the presentation of the Council of Europe's Diploma. The successful integration of the islanders' lifestyle with conservation of landscape and wildlife, for which the Diploma was awarded, is a concept very much in line with George's dreams for the island, dreams which he was lucky enough to see largely fulfilled during his lifetime. It is appropriate that his efforts on the island's behalf are now commemorated in the George Waterston Memorial Centre as well as the Bird Observatory.

Like many of the beneficial changes that have taken place on Fair Isle in the last 40 years, the museum development came about only through co-operation between, and contributions from, a variety of bodies. The National Trust for Scotland, as landlord, has played a vital part in most of the improvements. Financial support has come from Shetland Islands Council, government bodies such as the Highlands and Islands Development Board and the Countryside Commission for Scotland and charitable trusts. And the islanders themselves have provided not only the impetus towards achieving targets but also much time and labour and often astonishingly large cash contributions for such a small community. One result of all this co-operative effort is that, in the words of the Council of Europe's booklet, 'No longer is Fair Isle an isolated island, physically or socially, but rather a place where islanders can live a hard but satisfactory life, away from the less attractive aspects of the modern world outside, and where visitors can be revitalised by the beauty of the island and its birds, and by the spirit of its inhabitants'.

CHAPTER TEN

Birds, at all Seasons

The variety of migrant birds making landfall on Fair Isle continues to excite and intrigue today's birdwatchers, as it did Eagle Clarke and the Duchess of Bedford earlier this century. One of the attractions is that birds rarely seen in Britain, and originating from all points of the compass, not infrequently turn up on the island. Of the 340 species recorded by the end of 1988, only 35 are residents or regular summer visitors which breed every year. Most of the others are pausing on a long journey to rest and feed on this speck of land surrounded by inhospitable sea. Where are they coming from and going to? And why should birds from places as far apart as Siberia and North America arrive on Fair Isle? These are the main questions for which migration studies seek to find answers. Bird-ringing is an important tool in this work, and also provides information on subjects such as life expectancy and journey time. And when birds are caught for ringing there is opportunity to investigate weights and measurements, plumage colour and moulting patterns, and parasite burdens. But first, of course, the bird must be identified.

Until the 1930s identification of unusual species always involved 'obtaining' the bird, as sight records were considered unreliable, but by the time Fair Isle Bird Observatory was established trapping had replaced shooting — though as late as 1952 one elderly visitor, a member of the old school who had come armed with a walking-stick gun, caused consternation by producing from his pocket the corpse of a bird whose identity was under debate! Most birds are still caught in big wire-netting funnel traps of the type developed more than half a century ago at the Heligoland migration station, but over the years other capture methods have also been tried. Using bright torchlight to dazzle roosting waders and catching small birds in flight in a very fine-mesh 'mist' net are among the most successful of these. Once caught the bird is taken back to the observatory, where it is examined in as much detail as may be necessary to confirm its identification, then weighed, measured, ringed and, where possible, aged and sexed before being released.

For most of the commoner migrants identification is no problem, though notes of weights, measurements and plumage tones are often worth recording as they can help to indicate which area a bird has come from; wheatears from Greenland, for example, are bigger and more brightly coloured than those breeding in Shetland. But for less familiar species, and especially those seldom if ever previously recorded in Britain, it is necessary to note detailed descriptions of as many aspects as possible of the bird's appearance, both in the hand and when it is at liberty. Such notes are of value not only in ensuring that a record is accepted by the committees which maintain the official list of 'British birds' but also for helping others to identify the species if it turns up again somewhere else in Britain.

The sporadic arrival of species whose normal haunts may lie thousands of kilometres from Britain was something which early workers on migration found hard to explain. Eagle Clarke believed that much of Fair Isle's importance as a migration station was due to its position 'in the flightline of hosts of migrants' — in other words, that a route via the Northern Isles was deliberately followed by large numbers of Scandinavian-breeding birds, as well as by those travelling to and from Iceland and Greenland. He claimed that American species arriving in Britain 'doubtless reach us after having travelled by way of Greenland, Iceland and the Faroes' and considered that the appearance of vagrants, which he referred to as waifs, was 'in most instances due to the errors or indiscretions of youth; they have failed to follow the right course leading to the usual winter retreats'. Although accepting that in some cases these waifs might have been overtaken by adverse weather and driven off their course, he believed that as a general rule wind direction affected only the start of migration.

A rather different view was developed by the Misses Baxter and Rintoul, as a result of their studies on the Isle of May. In 1918 they wrote 'There are strong grounds for believing that the route followed by birds on migration depends largely on the direction of the wind. . . . We believe that deviation from the direct route is perhaps mainly due to drift'. Since over-sea flights must be the most hazardous for small land birds, it seemed to them obvious that preferred routes would wherever possible be over land; if this were true then Scandinavian migrants arriving on British shores, instead of flying directly south towards Africa overland, must do so as a result of being blown off-course. So began the theory of migrational drift which was to be the focus of Kenneth Williamson's work at Fair Isle Bird Observatory.

Ringing is an important tool in the study of bird migration, for which Fair Isle is well-known. Most of the birds ringed are caught in Heligoland traps; many 'rarities' have been captured in this one, at the Gully.

In developing the migrational drift theory, Ken correlated meteorological records with migrant arrivals and concluded that it should be possible, given knowledge of prevailing weather conditions, both to predict when large 'falls' of birds would reach British shores and to identify their likely area of origin. Migrating birds are greatly influenced by two distinct types of weather. Most prefer to start their journey when clear skies enable them to orientate by sun or stars, and when light or tail winds make flying easy; these conditions usually prevail in or close to areas of high pressure, around which winds blow in a clockwise direction. They may fail to follow their intended route if bad weather with poor visibility causes them to become disorientated, or when strong cross winds make it impossible for them to maintain direction; such conditions often arise in low pressure areas — the deeper the depression, the stronger the anti-clockwise winds around it and the stormier the fronts associated with it.

When large numbers of Scandinavian birds reach Fair Isle in autumn there has most probably been high pressure over Norway, to get them going, and a depression somewhere in southern Britain, producing strong south-easterly or easterly winds which deflected, or drifted, them across the North Sea as they flew southwards. Different locations for the high and low pressure areas are obviously involved during spring migration, but the principle (though much simplified here) is the same, and the same general pattern of events is also responsible for bringing many of the vagrants from much further afield. Finally, the weather over Fair Isle must be clear enough for the birds to see the island itself, the breaking seas that fringe it, or — especially important for the many small night migrants — the beams of one of the lighthouses. If they fail to locate this landfall the birds are likely to go on travelling with the wind, since this taxes their strength less than trying to fly against it, and risk being carried far out into the Atlantic. Many must, in fact, come to grief in this way.

By studying developing weather patterns in spring and autumn ornithologists can often anticipate when the next day's birdwatching is likely to be exciting. On such occasions the enthusiasts are up at dawn, driving the traps and walking the island to identify and count the birds that have touched down during the night or are arriving as the sky clears. Sometimes it is the sheer numbers that are impressive. On 3rd May 1969, for example, arrivals included some 300 ring ouzels, 45 wrynecks, 400 willow warblers, 500 bramblings, 32 ortolan buntings and at least 1,500 tree pipits. An enormous fall on 22nd September 1981 involved an estimated 1000 blackcaps and 400 garden warblers, with smaller numbers of siskins, swallows, little stints, mealy redpolls and both ortolan and snow buntings. During October several thousand redwings and fieldfares, and hundreds of blackbirds and song thrushes, are often on the island at one time. But for many birdwatchers it is quality rather than quantity that gives the greatest thrill.

For those keen to extend their 'life list' the variety of species occurring on the island is a special draw, as is the possibility of being present when a new bird for Britain is first recorded. Fair Isle's register of 'first records' is an impressive one, with no fewer than 17 'new for Britain' species since the Observatory was established, and a further 15 'firsts for Scotland' in the same period. Many of these unusual visitors are small passerines, such as pipits, warblers and buntings, but they also include occasional wildfowl, waders and birds of prey. A few are species which breed in western Europe or around the Mediterranean, but the majority of the 'firsts' started their journey in either Central Asia/Siberia or North America.

One of the joys of spring migration is that the birds are in breeding plumage, the males in particular often living up to their text book representations. Bluethroats, with a central red spot setting off the vivid blue bib, and immaculately marked bramblings and Lapland buntings, are perhaps the most decorative of the Scandinavian breeders that pass through in varying numbers. Scarlet rosefinches are among the species from slightly further east which not infrequently over-shoot while on spring migration, perhaps swept along by warm easterlies, to appear well to the north and west of their breeding range. Also in this group are several Fair Isle specialities, such as thrush nightingale, river warbler, and greenish warbler, which breed still further east. In some years birds from southern Europe and the Mediterranean basin appear — for example, lesser kestrel, bee-eater, red-rumped swallow, short-toed lark, black-eared wheatear and subalpine warbler — and there have even been occurrences of such normally sedentary species as Sardinian warbler.

In addition to Continental vagrants from widely scattered areas, spring also occasionally sees the arrival of waders and landbirds from America. Three of the four species of American sparrows recorded on Fair Isle have appeared in spring, as have yellow-rumped warbler, hermit thrush, American kestrel and sandhill crane. But in both spring and autumn transatlantic vagrants are, not surprisingly, much scarcer than those from Eurasia.

September and October are the peak months for autumn 'specials'. Due partly to the large numbers of young birds making their first migratory journey, and partly to the periodic build-up of high pressure over Siberia, there is a likelihood of unusual visitors from far to the east turning up at this season. Olive-backed, Pechora and Richard's pipits, all Siberian breeders, occur more frequently on Fair Isle than anywhere else in Britain. Among the eastern warblers Pallas's grasshopper and lanceolated are Fair Isle specialities; arctic and yellow-browed occur almost annually; Pallas's and paddyfield have been recorded several times; and there are records of dusky, Radde's and thick-billed (a first for Europe when it was identified in 1955). Many of these autumn migrants are birds of the year and have not yet achieved adult plumage, which makes their identification even more difficult; the Siberian rubythroat which arrived in October 1975, for example, lacked any trace of the colourful plumage which gives the species its name.

These rarer visitors are usually few and far between and have to be 'worked for' by careful examination of any bird which looks a bit different. Just occasionally, however, a really exceptional group of species is present at one time, as on 1st and 2nd October 1987. The migration log for those dates included Richard's and olive-backed pipits (W Siberia/NE Russia), rustic and little buntings (NE Europe), Radde's and yellow-browed warblers (Central Asia/Siberia), red-breasted flycatcher (E Europe) and Scotland's first savannah sparrow, from America. It is occasions like this which sustain Fair Isle's reputation as an outstanding place for seeing unusual vagrant birds.

Although spring and autumn are the most exciting periods for the

Birds reach Fair Isle from many different directions, often blown far from their normal haunts. This hoopoe (*above*) had overshot its breeding range in mainland Europe, while the white-crowned sparrow had been drifted right across the Atlantic.

migrant watcher, they are by no means the only times when unexpected birds appear. Late autumn has seen dusky warbler, dotterel and white-tailed eagle as highlights among the regular falls of woodcock and passage of geese and snow buntings; in midwinter Iceland gulls and little auks occur annually, with ivory gull and gyrfalcon putting in an occasional appearance; and the only Fair Isle great bustard arrived in mid January 1970. In early spring the crescendo of migration starts with Lapland and snow buntings, and waders, followed by thrushes and chats; and even in the migration 'doldrums' of July and early August one of the scarcer sandpipers or an irruption of crossbills sometimes enlivens the scene. But midsummer is really a time for seabird watching, when the island is alive with the unceasing noise and movement of the breeding colonies.

Though migration studies are still an important facet of the ornithological work on Fair Isle, the island's seabird populations have recently attracted an increasing proportion of the Bird Observatory's attention. These populations are the primary reason for the island's designation as a Site of Special Scientific Interest and its inclusion in the Nature Conservation Review, which lists the most important natural history sites in Britain. No fewer than 17 of Britain's 24 breeding seabird species are represented among the 90,000 or so pairs currently nesting on Fair Isle. Monitoring of the seabirds, to check on any population changes which may be taking place, now forms a major part of the Observatory's summer work and is helping to expand understanding of the factors affecting seabird numbers.

Fair Isle's seabirds fascinate by their very numbers, their varied lifestyles, and the astonishing changes their populations have undergone this century. Throughout the breeding season blizzards of birds hurtle across, or ride on, the aerial currents along cliff faces thronged with nests, which range from the kittiwake's carefully constructed cup of weed and mud to the bare ledges occupied by guillemots. Arctic and great skuas patrol territories scattered over much of the moorland interior, and parades of puffins stand sentry beside their underground nests. These, and the big gulls, are the most obvious of the island's seabirds; the others are either scarcer or less obtrusive. Many of the shags nest in caves, the razorbills and black guillemots occupy crevices and crannies among the rocks, the colonies of terns, gannets and common gulls are small, and the storm petrels emerge from their burrows only at dusk. Although many of these species have probably bred on Fair Isle for centuries, several have established colonies only in the relatively recent past, among them the now ubiquitous fulmar.

Eagle Clarke recorded that fulmars were present all summer for the first time in 1902, bred in 1903 and 10 years later were nesting 'in all suitable places round the island'. Between 1912 and 1975 a population explosion took place, occupied sites increasing to an estimated 3000 by 1959 and 26,000 in 1975. Since then the expansion has slowed down, with the 1986 figure only 4% up on 1975, probably because all suitable places on the cliffs really are now fully occupied. In the past fulmars were absent for about three months during autumn and winter but now they desert the cliffs for only a few days in autumn; it is suspected that this behavioural change, too, may be a result of the current pressure on space. As the most abundant of the island's seabirds the fulmar inevitably has an impact on other species, perhaps most clearly on any predators misguided enough to assess it as an easy meal. A well-aimed defensive jet of fishy oil is not only an effective deterrent at the time but may also have a more lasting effect through contamination of the attacking bird's plumage, which can render it unable to fly. The fact that a young Norwegian white-tailed eagle hand-reared and released on the isle in 1968 suffered this fate highlights one ecological effect of changing seabird populations; when sea eagles formerly lived on Fair Isle they were not exposed to this particular risk as there were no fulmars for them to prey on.

At the present time Fair Isle's gannet colony, one of Scotland's newest, is undergoing rapid expansion. Between 1975, when chicks were first hatched, and 1988 the number of nests increased from eight to more than 488, occupying no fewer than eight separate sites. With as many as 2000, including many immature non-breeders, coming ashore on the west coast, the sight of plunge-diving gannets has become a regular and pleasant feature of island seabird watching. While numbers remain manageably small, the nesting gannets will be counted annually, as are the breeding skuas, terns and common gulls. But censusing the populations of the more abundant, and in some cases less accessible, species is an even more difficult and time-consuming task, requiring calm weather for counts from seaward of cliff sections not visible from above.

The breeding seabirds, other than storm petrels, were counted for the first time in 1969, but were not comprehensively censused again until 1986, when a nation-wide survey was mounted by the Nature Conservancy Council. It is intended in future to re-census two or three species annually in each five-year period, and to complement this overall population monitoring with detailed studies carried out every year in selected areas. Annual nest counts show up any sudden marked population change; the number of chicks reared per nest gives a measure of productivity; weights and wing lengths indicate chick growth rates — which reflect food availability; sample collection allows the most important foods to be identified; and checking for birds carrying a combination of colour rings specific to a particular year enables adult survival to be assessed.

Over the years the results of comprehensive monitoring on Fair Isle, together with data from other seabird colonies, should help to shed light on many aspects of seabird population dynamics. Will the increase seen in most species during the last few decades continue? Or will numbers start to decline again, as those of shag and the three big gulls did on Fair Isle between 1975 and 1986? And if they do, will it be possible to identify the cause? Even short-term studies can highlight the effects of weather on chick survival in some species — in 1987, for example, the 350 pairs of terns nesting on the isle failed to rear a single chick due to wet weather in July — but only long-term studies will be able to confirm or contradict the current theory that commercial fishing of sandeels, the most important food for young seabirds, must inevitably have an adverse impact on seabird populations.

Research workers from many parts of Britain take advantage of another side of Fair Isle's ornithological interest — the fact that its relatively small size and isolated position make it a convenient site for studying individual species. Studies extending over many years and carried out largely by visiting ornithologists have provided fascinating insights into widely differing aspects of the life of Fair Isle's own race of wren, the local starlings — believed to be largely sedentary, and the colony of arctic skuas, which expanded from a mere 15 breeding pairs in 1949 to a peak of 180 pairs in 1969-70.

It was Ken Williamson who recognised that Fair Isle wrens were sufficiently different from those breeding in Shetland to merit their own subspecific status, and named the race *Troglodytes troglodytes fridariensis*, from the Fridarey of the Orkneyinga Saga. *Fridariensis* resembles the Shetland race in being bigger than the UK mainland wren, but differs from it in colour, being a paler and brighter brown above, more reddish on the rump, and less heavily marked below. Its song is more musical and even louder and more vigorous than that of mainland birds, but slower and less varied. Spectogram analyses of tape recordings made 11 years apart show a remarkable similarity in phrasing, with a distinctive 'weedle-weedle' repeated three or four times near both beginning and end of each song cycle, a characteristic not recorded in wren song from other parts of Britain.

The tiny size of the Fair Isle wren population prompted the International Council for Bird Preservation to include it in their Red Data Book of Endangered Species, the only British bird species which qualifies for inclusion. Counts of singing males have ranged between 50+ in the early 1960s and an all-time low of only 10 in 1981 — fortunately followed by a progressive recovery to 30 in 1987. With such a

The island's important breeding seabird population includes a flourishing colony of great skuas, or bonxies as they are called in Shetland. These piratical birds are sometimes unpopular with both visitors and islanders as they dive-bomb intruders on their territory.

small population one might think it easy to carry out a full census, but this is far from being the case. In the nesting season Fair Isle wrens are cliff-birds, especially favouring geos with stony beaches on which wreaths of tideline wrack ensure abundant insect food. In such situations wind, waves and seabirds frequently combine to make even vociferous small birds like wrens difficult to hear. Their song must necessarily be loud for them to have much prospect of attracting a mate! Unlike their mainland counterparts, the island wrens appear to be strictly monogamous, which probably helps chick survival as both parents are able to give undivided attention to their brood. Fair Isle is only rarely subjected to heavy snow cover or sub-zero temperatures, the factors responsible for massive drops in mainland wren populations, yet island numbers occasionally undergo dramatic declines, for example the 50% decrease recorded between 1978 and 1979. Wet and windy winters have been suggested as one possible explanation, while poor summer weather doubtless has an adverse effect on chick survival. Probably a combination of factors is involved, but further investigation will be necessary before these fluctuations can be fully understood.

Study of individual starlings' life histories is simplified by the fact that many of those on Fair Isle nest in drystone dykes, where they are relatively easily accessible for ringing and examination. The island population has been extensively colour-ringed since 1981 and it is planned soon also to employ 'genetic finger-printing', a scientific technique used by the police and based on the fact that every individual has a unique combination of genetic material, and closely related individuals show more similarities than do randomly selected members of a mixed population. Examination of blood samples from Fair Isle starlings has demonstrated that the frequency of particular genes is very different from that in starlings from other areas, supporting the view that the population is a self-contained one. Doubts have, however, recently been raised as to whether this is in fact the case. Many young starlings leave the island in autumn but it was believed that they returned there to breed — until a colour-ringed bird was found breeding in Orkney. Future results should shed light on this question.

The information obtained by colour-marking has already high-lighted certain strange aspects of the starling's domestic life. Some females lay in another's nest, usually one with which they have had an earlier association, often through being reared there. And some males practise infanticide, visiting a neighbour's nest and pecking the chicks to death.

Domestic affairs have been the focus of long-term studies in the arctic skua colony too. In this case one aim was to elucidate the inheritance of the three distinct colour phases — pale, intermediate and dark — and another to investigate breeding details, such as age at first breeding, fidelity, and incubation and fledging periods. Colour-ringing was again the key to this work, enabling life histories of individual birds to be compiled over a period of years. So that data collection would be as rapid as possible adults were marked as well as chicks, which involved catching them on the nest — a process requiring great patience on the part of the operator. After substituting a hard-boiled egg for the skua's own, the catcher retreated into a hide to wait until the bird returned; once it had settled a quick yank to the string attached to a flip-over net usually resulted in a capture. Although some individuals were so aware of the human presence that they persistently dive-bombed the hide, not a single one deserted as a result of this indignity. And the technique even worked with a pair that was optimistically incubating an old cartridge case! They were subsequently rewarded with a foster chick, which they reared successfully.

Over the years many birdwatchers have been attracted to Fair Isle by its reputation as a migration station, while others have taken advantage of the facilities provided by the Bird Observatory in carrying out ornithological studies of widely differing kinds. It is to be hoped that many more will do so in the years ahead — and that researchers will also take the opportunity to study other aspects of the island's wildlife. The scope for such studies is considerable.

CHAPTER ELEVEN

Other Creatures, Great and Small

Although best known in natural history circles for its birds, Fair Isle also possesses a good variety of other wildlife interest, both botanical and zoological; and there is almost certainly much still to be discovered, as comparatively few detailed non-ornithological studies have yet been made. The island's lack of habitat diversity — a feature closely linked to island size, and its separation by 25 miles of sea from its nearest neighbours, are reflected in the limited variety of both plants and animals, but both groups nevertheless include species which are noteworthy in a Shetland context.

Botanically, the interest stretches back some 350 million years, to the Middle Devonian period, when Fair Isle was part of a land mass which linked Scotland with Norway, Greenland and America. Fossil plants of that period preserved in the island's sandstones are yielding information of interest not only for itself but also for its potential value in oil exploration. The fossils described from sites near Slogar on Buness and at Roskilie are, respectively, a 3-4 metre high plant with woody stem and crown of fern-like foliage (which occurs also in Spitzbergen), and an even more primitive dumpy bush; both are present in a reproductive state, bearing spore-cases.

Unlike these predecessors, the spore-bearing plants on the island today are mainly small and relatively fragile, with bracken standing out for its vigour and hardiness. Most of the other ferns have been recorded only in rocky crevices, on sea cliffs or in moist sheltered spots such as the Gully, but the delicate Wilson's filmy fern also grows on Ward Hill, while the inconspicuous little stems of moonwort and adder's tongue are thinly scattered in several dry grassland areas. Studies of mosses and liverworts carried out in September 1986 added some 46 new species to the Fair Isle list, bringing the total recorded to more than 80.

There have been recent additions to the fungus list too, one of the new

Many fewer flowering plants grow on Fair Isle than on the Shetland mainland, but there are likely to be some present which have not yet been recorded. The round-leaved sundew is one of the most recent additions to the local list.

records being a first for Britain. Some of the fungi growing on the island occur also in Scandinavia and the Faroes, and several are closely associated with such specialised habitats as rabbit or sheep droppings, or the ground-hugging 'forests' of creeping and least willow. The absence of true woodland, with its accompanying dead wood and leaf litter, greatly restricts the range of fungi and lichens able to grow on the island. When the most complete list of Fair Isle's lichens yet published was compiled in 1961 the trees in the Vaadal 'forest' were too young to harbour lichens, but by 1988 those most exposed to the weather carried a quite extensive lichen flora. Fence posts often support several lichen species, but the two most significant habitats for this group are soil, especially where it is peaty, and rocks, both near the shoreline and on drier inland sites such as dykes and buildings.

Also included in the category of flowerless plants are the seaweed communities of the shoreline, which vary in composition with exposure to wave action. Although the tidal range on Fair Isle is only about 2-3 metres, on exposed stretches of coast the spray of breaking waves continually wets the rocks more than a metre above high water mark

even on a calm day, and occasionally splashes even higher. This constant
wetting, together with the generally high humidity, allows seaweeds and
limpets to flourish much further above high tide line on such coasts than
in sheltered sites — and consequently makes landings on Sheep Craig
somewhat hazardous. The most comprehensive survey of the island's
marine biology carried out to date was made in 1987, when examination
of sites scattered widely around the coast confirmed the variety of
shoreline communities available for study. An arctic species of wrack is
one of the leathery seaweeds that flourish on the most exposed sites,
while bristle-worms, sea-mats and 'dead men's fingers' occur among the
widespread 'forests' of coralline algae. The Tail o' Uren, off Skadan, is an
especially interesting site, combining as it does both very exposed shore
and areas of localised shelter.

Fair Isle's flowering plants number less than half those recorded for
Shetland as a whole (some 240+ species as against around 600), due
partly to physical influences and partly to man's use of the land. The
generally acid soils, long history of heavy grazing by sheep, and almost
universal effects of wind and salt-spray are the main factors responsible
for the limited variety of the island's present-day plant life. In some
places local concentrations of bird droppings have so enriched the soil
that the resultant vivid green growth stands out in contrast to nearby
vegetation. And where sheltered crevices and gullies provide protection
from wind-blast, and steep rocky faces from grazing sheep, the plant life
is both lusher and more varied. But these mitigating influences have little
or no effect over most of the isle, the uncultivated portion of which is
predominantly dwarf-shrub moorland, interspersed with damp areas
which support a rather limited range of bog plants. The remaining
unimproved grassland is typical of acid soils, with fescues, tormentil and
woodrush, while salt-tolerant species such as thrift, sea plantain, buck's-
horn plantain and spring squill dominate the short coastal sward.

All Fair Isle's 'trees' are diminutive, some naturally and some by force
of circumstance. The native creeping willow, which clings closely to
roadside banks near Field and Stackhoull, and the least willow, growing
near the summit of Ward Hill, both spread horizontally, relying on
underground rhizomes rather than trunks. Tree species which lack such
adaptations for survival in hard conditions suffer so badly from wind-
blast and salt spray that their growth is stunted, even in what appears to
be a relatively sheltered spot. The Vaadal 'forest' of Sitka spruce and
sycamore was planted in the 1950s but after more than 30 years growth
has attained a height of little more than 3 metres; in more favourable
conditions these trees would by now be at least 15 metres high.

Dwarfness is also a characteristic of the moorland vegetation, a wind-clipped mat of low twisted stems of heather, bell heather, crowberry and prostrate juniper — the last a species now scarce elsewhere in Shetland. The ground beneath has been impoverished by past 'scalping' of turf and is often bare peat, or patchily covered with lichens, but in some places there are colonies of tiny heath spotted-orchids and lesser twayblade, and in Wirvie Brecks the white stars of chickweed wintergreen show briefly in early summer, here in very different surroundings from its original woodland habitat. Such typical mountain species as alpine bistort and stiff sedge grow on Ward Hill, occasional plants of sea campion occur far inland, and mini versions of the slender St John's wort, which reaches normal size in the shelter of Finniquoy, also cower among the heather. But few of the more colourful flowers are present in sufficient numbers, or are large enough, to stand out against the predominantly purple-tawny colour which the shrubs, grasses and sedges give to the moorland and the grassier heath.

Some of the island's scarcest and most interesting plants occur in the boggy moorland and rough grassland areas. Marsh willowherb, though quite common, is of interest in that it is one of the species found also in Greenland and North America, and because on Fair Isle it occurs in both semi-double-flowered and white forms as well as the more usual pink. Lesser marshwort, a rare plant in Shetland, grows in the Gilsetter Burn, and the tiny pink-flowered bog pimpernel, which is also very local, bloomed profusely at several sites in 1982 and 1988. Both dates and abundance of flowering vary from one season to another with many species according to climatic conditions, while just how great an effect changes in management can have on the grassland flora was demonstrated recently on croft ground which had traditionally been grazed by sheep and cattle. When Shetland botanist Walter Scott prepared his 'Checklist of the Flora of Fair Isle', published in 1971, he commented that the occurrence of the northern marsh orchid required confirmation; in 1986 no fewer than 228 spikes were counted on a single July day, in an area left ungrazed.

The most reliably profuse flowering, however, takes place on the cliffs, where plants can flourish in spots safe from the attentions of the sheep — which on Fair Isle means only in really inaccessible clefts and ledges. In such places red campion, kidney vetch and bird's-foot trefoil add their splashes of colour to the pink of thrift and white of sea campion. In a few places there are clumps of roseroot, Scots lovage and wild angelica, sprays of scentless mayweed, and tufts of spiny spear thistle. And here and there a cluster of primroses is tucked into a really sheltered damp crevice. Against the generally muted colours of the rock, and of the dominant island vegetation, these floral highlights seem especially bright, as do the very local inland clumps of marsh marigold and meadowsweet, which stand out for their vivid colour and relative height respectively.

There is probably much still to be discovered about the island's flowering plants. Walter Scott drew attention to some apparent 'absentees', native species occurring in comparable habitats elsewhere in Shetland but not yet recorded on Fair Isle. Only one of these, the insectivorous sundew, has since been located. Are some of the others perhaps still waiting to be found? And what about those which, like the northern marsh orchid, Scott recorded as 'requiring confirmation', either because they have not been found for many years or because the original identification was open to doubt? Although some of these require specialist knowledge for certain identification this is not true of all; anyone should be able to spot a wild rose, the only record of which dates from 1917.

As with plants, the variety of 'native' invertebrate species is evidently limited — though as yet studies have been far from comprehensive. Among insects, the fleas and other parasites carried by birds received a good deal of attention in the Observatory's early years, and there have been periodic, usually short-term, surveys of beetles and Lepidoptera. Spiders, slugs and snails have been reported on as a result of brief collecting forays, but records for most other groups, including marine molluscs and crustaceans, have been only casual ones obtained in the course of other work. But despite its sketchiness, the information available on these lowly creatures serves to focus attention on several points of interest in relation to the island's populations.

What, for example, is the significance of the fact that only single specimens of certain insect species have been found? Does it just mean that they are relatively scarce residents, or does it imply that they are casual visitors; and if the latter, how did they reach the island? Where bird parasites are concerned the answer seems obvious, and is supported by such findings as the first records for Britain of two ticks, one on a rose-coloured starling from south-east Europe and the other on an American grey-cheeked thrush. And strong-flying insects, such as the common aeshna dragonfly seen in August 1955, the red admiral and painted lady butterflies which occasionally appear, and some of the larger beetles, doubtless reached the island by a combination of wing and wind power. But quite a number of the species recorded are flightless or have only rudimentary wings. Noting that of 14 species collected only two were regular fliers, and a further two or three able only to rise more or less accidentally into the air, one scientist has suggested two possible

Wind and salt spray have a marked effect on the island's plant life, much of which is dwarfer in form than it would be under less harsh conditions. These Sitka spruces in Vaadal plantation are not much over 3m high after more than 30 years growth.

explanations: either this is the result of genetic selection towards flightless forms, or some species have reached the island by means other than flight.

In view of the limited range of habitats, and the relative scarcity of succulent leafy vegetation, it is perhaps hardly surprising that many of the 70+ beetle species are carnivorous, as are the 60+ spiders. The majority of the beetles recorded on Fair Isle are widely distributed on the mainland but a few are characteristic of mountain and moorland areas. So, too, is the wolf spider reckoned to be the most abundant invertebrate on the island, a species apparently confined to the heather areas and occurring in similar situations in Iceland and Greenland. The heather moorland also supports substantial populations of noctuid moths, the caterpillars of which are an important spring source of food for the island's mice as well as for birds. The large day-flying moths typical of mainland moors, the emperor and northern eggar, are absent, however, although the emperor is common in Orkney.

A mercury vapour trap is currently yielding much new information on the isle's resident and migrant moths. August seems to be a peak month for emergence of the commoner species, and at least the occasional migrant is still around as late as November. Many, but by no means all, individuals of the resident species are dark in colour and represent the variants typical of the Northern Isles. Trapping results suggest that the Fair Isle list of 'macro moths' is a short one, illustrating yet again the effect of isolation on some of the island's populations.

Information on insect groups other than those already mentioned is still scarce. The sole representative of the bee family on Fair Isle, as elsewhere in Shetland, is the reddish local variety of bumble bee; two species of ant are known to occur; and a small bristle-tail or thrips is very abundant among loose material along the cliff edge. An absentee that nobody regrets is the blow fly which is such a pest further south, both around the house and among sheep.

Apart from the 1987 survey little systematic attention has been given to shoreline molluscs and crustaceans, despite the opportunities presented by the tidal pools at the south end of the island, or to other marine invertebrates. From deeper water there are records of two species of squat lobster and a small spider crab, all caught in lobster creels during the spring of 1967, but with the reduction in lobster fishing this potential source of further information has gone. Additions to the very incomplete information on these groups will surely be dependent upon visiting specialists.

Fair Isle's resident, non-domestic, non-avian vertebrate list comprises a mere four species: field mouse, house mouse, rabbit and grey seal. Frogs have been introduced – as tadpoles for school study – but did not survive, and a pipistrelle was found clinging to a wall at the south end in June 1961, after a spell of southerly winds. But the only non-residents recorded at all regularly are marine mammals seen in the seas around the isle or from the *Good Shepherd* on the crossing from Grutness.

Of the resident species the field mouse is the most important, as it is sufficiently distinct to merit subspecific status. *Apodemus sylvaticus fridariensis*, intermediate in size between the mainland and St Kilda forms, was first described and named in 1906, and, unlike some others, has stood the test of time as a 'good' subspecies. The bulk of the field mouse population inhabits the moorland area, feeding mainly by night and using a criss-cross system of runways beneath the concealing canopy of the heather. Specimens caught in spring had been feeding mainly on animal foods, such as caterpillars, but grasses and seeds probably form a larger part of the diet in autumn and winter, when the mice tend to come in to the vicinity of the Observatory and the more northerly crofts. It is not entirely clear why they should avoid much of the village area, where they are replaced by the relatively restricted population of markedly smaller house mice, but the availability of cover, the presence of

The area around the 'feelie' dykes is much favoured by the island's multi-coloured rabbits. Even where the dykes have been levelled, in the course of agricultural improvement, the ground where they stood continues to offer good burrowing conditions.

predators, both avian and feline, and competition with house mice and rabbits are thought to be important factors in determining their distribution.

Ken Williamson believed that the small burrows he found on Sheep Craig were inhabited by field mice, but this theory has not yet been either proved or disproved. If it should be true the 'Rock' mice occupy a very different habitat from that of their relatives on the 'mainland' of Fair Isle. Instead of heather for cover there is only grass, though certainly this is notably long and lush, especially now that the sheep have been taken off. The food sources must be different, too, as the spring supply of noctuid caterpillars is likely to be negligible; perhaps the bundles of fishbones cast up by gulls provide a useful source of protein and minerals. So far as a mouse is concerned, Sheep Craig is effectively isolated from the main island, so a population living there would have to be self-contained, implying in-breeding and, through survival of the fittest, selection towards the mouse type best able to cope with these particular conditions.

Field mice are thought to have reached Fair Isle in Viking times, travelling from Norway to Shetland, and thence in due course to the isle, probably as uninvited hangers-on when settlers were transporting stock-feed and bedding. Fortunately for the many ground-nesting birds, those other ship-borne travellers the rats are absent — which seems rather surprising in view of the many shipwrecks in bygone days. Rabbits, on the other hand, must have been deliberately introduced. They are known to have been established in Shetland by the mid-17th century and were doubtless brought from there to Fair Isle with the aim of adding to the food supply. Today they are widely scattered but most abundant near the cliff tops and in the vicinity of the old feelie dykes, both situations which offer good burrowing conditions. They come in a wide range of colours, including black, white, ginger and white collared. Myxomatosis has never reached Fair Isle, despite the fact that it was widespread in Orkney in the 1960s, and the only direct threats to the rabbits come from man, his cats and dogs, and predatory birds such as skuas and gulls which occasionally take young ones. None of these seems likely to have a very significant influence on the size of the population, which is probably limited by winter food supply.

Unlike the rabbits, the local grey seals no longer attract man's predatory attentions. Seals were originally of value for their meat, oil and skins, but in the more recent past it was young pups that were taken, at an early age, for their white pelts, which commanded a good price. Officially, the hunting of grey seals has required a permit since 1914, but it was not until the introduction of more stringent protective legislation in 1970 that the practice entirely ceased on Fair Isle. Common seals, although abundant elsewhere in Shetland, are seldom seen on the island, which lacks the sheltered bays and low hauling out places preferred by this species.

The local grey seal population is believed to number somewhere in the region of 300. There are nearly always some to be seen off the west coast, especially near the Stacks of Skroo, and around Buness and in the South Harbour. Even when mist conceals them from observers on the clifftop their presence is proclaimed by their 'singing', an eerie sound which it is easy to associate with tales of mermaids!

Most of the young are born in autumn, but white-coated pups have been found right through to April. Their nurseries are shadowy beaches and overhung ledges at the inner end of caves, where the young pups are safe from predators during the 3-4 weeks that must pass before they are able to go to sea. During this period the pup suckles frequently and grows at a remarkable rate; after a couple of weeks it begins to shed its fluffy white coat, and once moulting is complete it is abandoned by its mother and left to 'take the plunge' into life at sea on its own. Not all pups reach this stage, however. Caves may provide protection from predators but they have their own in-built dangers; high seas, whipped up by an onshore gale, may sweep the pup out to sea or batter it against the rocks. Once safely away from land, grey seal calves disperse and often travel quite long distances within a few weeks. No tagging has been done on Fair Isle, but recoveries of animals marked at other colonies contribute towards understanding of the species' movements. In November 1961 two pups born on North Rona in the Western Isles reached Fair Isle when only 6-8 weeks old, having travelled some 150 miles in their first month at sea.

Fair Isle's grey seal pups are generally born in caves or on beaches not visible from above, so few visitors have a chance to watch them at the attractive white-pelt stage. Once they have shed their 'baby' hair, as this one is doing, they go to sea independently and may travel long distances when only a few weeks old.

As interest in marine mammals increases, the list of species seen off-shore is gradually being added to. Apart from grey seals, those seen more or less regularly in Fair Isle waters are all cetaceans: whales, dolphins and porpoises. The most frequently identified are white-beaked and Risso's dolphins, which are often sighted on the crossing from Grutness; the former sometimes ride the *Good Shepherd*'s bow wave for several minutes at a time. Common or harbour porpoises, the smallest members of the family, are also seen quite often, sometimes in parties of up to 10 together, though there has recently been a decrease in sightings, possibly due to the decline in sandeels. This species is most likely to be in the Fair Isle area between August and mid winter. Bottle-nosed dolphins are scarcer and have only occasionally been seen near the island. Schools of pilot whales (also members of the dolphin family) sometimes come close in, as in January 1983, when 200+ were off the south end. This is the 'caain' whale which was formerly hunted by driving a school into shallow water until the unfortunate animals panicked and stranded themselves; little such hunting was ever done on Fair Isle, however, as the coastline is not suitable. Killer whales, too, belong to the dolphins and are among the species seen from the island, most often in August-September and seldom in groups of more than five or six.

Only two of the larger whales have so far been reported. Minke whales — formerly known as the lesser rorqual and measuring up to 10 metres in length — have been sighted on several occasions, usually single animals or pairs. And a solitary dead sperm whale was spotted from the *Good Shepherd* in June 1987. Lone males, which may be 15 metres long, apparently quite often leave the large herds which roam the warmer southern seas and travel north into arctic waters; presumably this was one such animal. Several further species have been recorded around Shetland, among them the northern bottlenose whale, so future cetacean-spotting may well add new names to the Fair Isle list.

Although the island's importance for the study of migrating birds has long been recognised, it is only within the last 30 years that 'official' action has been taken to protect Fair Isle's wider scientific interest. First, in 1961, came designation of the whole island by the Nature Conservancy as a Site of Special Scientific Interest. Problems can arise, however, if designation restricts a crofter's freedom to increase the productivity of his ground — and most of the island's inbye land has been so altered by agricultural use that it has long ceased to have more than very local botanical interest. When re-notification became necessary, with the passing of the 1981 Wildlife and Countryside Act, the opportunity was therefore taken to review the situation, and as a result the SSSI boundary was amended to cover only the coastline and the northern scattald; these are the areas which support the breeding seabirds, the endemic wrens and fieldmice, and the regionally significant vegetation types. The aim of SSSI designation is to ensure no action is taken which would destroy or endanger the wildlife interest, but some changes, such as draining and improving the quality of the grazing, can be implemented even within the SSSI area, through a management agreement between the Nature Conservancy Council and the island Grazings Committee.

Fair Isle's breeding seabirds, moorland and coastal heath were assessed as of national importance when the Nature Conservation Review was compiled in the 1970s, resulting in classification as a Grade 2 site. And the presence of the fossils referred to earlier means that the isle is also mentioned in the 1980s Geological Conservation Review, yet to be published. More recent legislation introduced by the European Economic Community seems likely to bring yet another designation, as a Specially Protected Area, that is one supporting significant populations of species which are either local or relatively scarce in the Community as a whole. And just to complete the spectrum, the island falls within the Shetland National Scenic Area identified by the Countryside Commission for Scotland in 1978.

On Fair Isle today we find, then, a wealth of wildlife interest and spectacular scenery, assiduously protected by a bevy of bureaucratic bodies, and a small but currently thriving community, dependent largely upon crofting and crafts, and struggling to ensure a future for its children. The award of the Council of Europe's Diploma in 1986 gave official recognition to the fact that the great natural history significance and the beauty of the island owe much to the islanders' attitude of respect and care for their natural heritage. It is vitally important that in the future this harmony between man and nature should continue, to the benefit of both.

CHAPTER TWELVE

Looking Towards 2000

Although lifestyles have changed greatly since the days when seabirds and fish provided the mainstay of the islanders' diet, the prosperity of Fair Isle's community is still to a large extent dependent upon its natural resources. The principal difference between past and present situations is that these resources are no longer utilised directly on the spot, but instead provide the vital anchorage for a chain of interdependence linking the island and the 'outside world'. Without Fair Isle's ornithological interest there would be no Bird Observatory. Without the Observatory there would be far fewer visitors — and the island would probably not have been taken into the care of the National Trust for Scotland. Without the visitors economic constraints would make it impracticable to run such frequent plane and boat services, marketing of produce and crafts would be more complicated and expensive, and opportunities for mixing with people from other environments and ways of life would be much restricted. And without the initiative of the National Trust for Scotland, and the co-operation and financial help of many 'outside' bodies, most of the amenities now enjoyed by the islanders would have been more difficult, and some perhaps impossible, to achieve. That community developments have taken place without significant adverse impact on the island's wildlife was the primary justification for the Council of Europe's Diploma award; that they should continue to co-exist without conflict must surely be a principal aim for the future.

It is not just island lifestyles which have altered during the past century, however. There has also been a major change in the extent to which the Fair Islanders make their own decisions about matters affecting their well-being. Only a hundred years ago it was the laird's prerogative to decree who should live where, what rent they should pay, and what value in shop goods should be set against payment in kind; the only options open were to abide by the laird's decisions or to leave the island.

The ability of *Good Shepherd IV* to handle virtually all domestic and crofting traffic not only makes life easier but also helps to keep freight costs down. All improvements in communications are important, as they make island life psychologically less isolated.

The passing of the Crofting Acts ameliorated conditions to some extent but, as in many other rural areas, relatively little changed until after the Second World War. By the early 1950s there was growing awareness of the widening gap between the standard of amenities available on the mainland and those on the isle, but neither laird nor crofters had the power or the cash to do much about it. Only ten years later the situation had taken a remarkable leap forward. National Trust for Scotland ownership, combined with the rapidly increasing availability of grant aid from a variety of sources, had brought all sorts of improvements and developments from the 'wishful thinking' category into the realm of the possible. At first the National Trust initiated most developments, and it still plays a leading role in many, but this responsibility is increasingly being taken over by the islanders themselves.

At the individual level, the crofter himself now decides what improvements he would like made to his home, and negotiates for whatever grant may be available to him either directly, if the house is his own, or in conjunction with the NTS, if he is a tenant. At the community level, decisions affecting the whole population are taken by the Fair Isle Committee, in which all adult islanders are entitled to participate; specific responsibilities relating to the management of the electricity supply and the common grazings are carried out by the elected Fair Isle Electricity Council and Grazings Committee respectively. And at local government level, an islander serves on South Dunrossness Community Council and the isle is represented at Islands Council meetings by the Councillor for Dunrossness.

The islanders' awareness that in future the fortunes of the community will be influenced as much by their own decisions as by outside forces is demonstrated by their request that the National Trust for Scotland should work with them in preparing a Management Plan to provide guidelines for policy-making. The maintenance of a viable community living in harmony with the natural environment is rated a top priority in the Plan, but agreement over this obviously desirable objective is not, of course, enough to ensure that it will be achieved. To support that overall aim more difficult decisions, regarding population size, new settlers, land allocation and visitor use, are needed. In some ways the situation on a small island like Fair Isle is similar to that in any other isolated community — survival of the community as a whole may have to take precedence over individual ambition.

At present (1988) the resident population numbers almost 70 (including the nurse and her family, the teacher and her family, and the full-time staff of the Bird Observatory). This figure also includes several young people who are absent for much of the year, attending either secondary school or some form of further education. There are currently 12 children at the Fair Isle school, but only two under school age. Eight islanders are pensioners or nearing pension age, and about 24 are between 30 and 50 years old. The Management Plan suggests an optimum population of 70-80 — but it is important, too, that the age distribution is kept in balance as far as is practicable. So, in encouraging new residents to settle on the island, it is clearly sensible to give preference to young couples or families. But what would be the prospects of accommodation and work for young people who might wish to settle on Fair Isle?

Of the 22 croft houses standing today, only five are unoccupied. Taft (the only one still displaying some of the original features, such as an open hearth), and Springfield were lived in until relatively recently but have not been modernised, while North Busta, Kennaby and Pund have lain derelict or ruinous for many years. The Haa, at one time by far the largest and most impressive house on the island, is about to be renovated and will shortly be available for letting, and there is one sheltered house not yet occupied. On the face of it, then, there is potential accommodation for another five or six families — with the possibility of National Trust assistance if the construction of a new house should be approved. But the

The craft co-operative provides flexible employment opportunities for both longstanding and incoming residents, and for both men and women. While building on the established reputation of Fair Isle pattern knitwear, it also offers scope for future expansion.

Haa has no croft land, only a garden; the former Pund, Kennaby and North Busta croft ground has been reallocated to others; and the new house 'Koolin' is now the homestead for the Springfield ground. For any new settlers to be provided with even a 10 acre croft would mean reducing the area available to existing residents, and with only three of the present units larger than 25 acres subdivision could be difficult. It is, however, the existence of a 'tie' to the land that is important nowadays,

For the future well-being of the island it is important that old traditions —
exemplified here by the native Shetland sheep — and new developments, such
as the Community Hall, blend together happily, as they have done to date.

rather than the ability of that land to make a significant contribution to
the occupants' livelihood, so croft size is no longer as critical a factor as it
once was.

Whereas accommodation might be available, earning a living is likely
to present bigger problems. One of the Management Plan's policy
statements is that new residents must be able to make a living without
prejudicing the employment of existing residents. In effect, this means

that none of the established back-up sources of income is likely to be available to new occupiers unless someone is willing either to retire or to resign from a paid occupation. As automation progressively decreases such traditional employment opportunities as lighthouse relief and coastguard duties — and it has already resulted in a decrease in the number of crew members needed to operate the *Good Shepherd* — regular work is increasingly hard to find. There are some jobs in connection with house construction and modernisation, road repairs, and so on, but these tend to be irregular or at best seasonal. Membership of the craft co-operative is open to anyone, and knitwear production, already a valuable source of income for many households, is capable of further expansion — but not all men fancy knitting as a main source of livelihood. It seems likely that individual initiative will play an increasing role in Fair Isle's economy in the future, the directions this might take naturally depending upon the interests and talents of the individuals concerned. Although the National Trust for Scotland can be expected to continue its supportive and catalytic role, future developments will inevitably be constrained by the island situation.

High freight costs mean that the import and export of bulky materials is best avoided. Any new venture will therefore need to involve either a high skill factor or a ready market actually on the island — or, better still, both. The recently reintroduced boat-building, which gives substantial added-value to materials brought in, meets the first of these criteria, as does violin-making, a craft at which another of the younger generation has already tried his hand. Where on-island sales are concerned, potential customers are limited to the community itself, the Observatory and visitors. There is considerable scope, at least during the summer months, for increased sales to the Lodge of home-produce, especially salad and root vegetables and perhaps eggs. One of George Waterston's ideas was for sunken vegetable gardens and protection would certainly be needed to provide shelter from the wind and encourage early growth, but the fact that under suitable conditions tomato plants on the isle will set fruits by mid-May suggests that some horticultural crops could do well. The results achieved in the trial polythene tunnel erected at Vaasetter in 1988 should indicate what may be practicable along these lines. Other possibilities might include the production of small souvenirs, such as models of straw-backed chairs or yoles, carvings displaying the graining patterns of the wood, sheepskin rugs and slippers, slide sets or mounted prints of the island — any items, in fact, likely to appeal to souvenir hunters looking for something as an alternative to knitwear.

Visitors, both residents at the hostel and those arriving on a more casual basis, like the 'adventure cruise' parties coming ashore by rubber dinghy, are likely to play an increasingly important role in Fair Isle's economy. Probably the most-needed addition to the amenities available to non-residents, and one likely to be well-used, is a source of light refreshments 'down the island'. Visitors are often invited into croft houses for a cup of tea, and they greatly appreciate this hospitality, but many would welcome the knowledge that refreshment could be obtained at appropriate times of day without dependence on a crofter's generosity. There may also be scope for expanding the services currently available to visitors in other ways. Boat trips around the island are already arranged on request, weather permitting; perhaps fishing trips, using traditional methods, might also have appeal. The wider the range of experiences that visitors can enjoy the greater the likelihood that they will report favourably on their visit — and there is no better publicity than that achieved by word of mouth.

There is, too, an ever-growing need for 'experts' resident on the island. In the increasingly technological society of today much depends upon the smooth-running not only of engines but also of such things as electronic controls — and to bring a specialist to Fair Isle to rectify a relatively minor fault can be an expensive business. The islanders have always been able to turn their hand to most of the traditional tasks — plumbing, joinery, building, and so on — but the skills necessary for coping with modern facilities cannot readily be learned on the spot.

Although not without practical problems, the computer age does open up opportunities for working at tasks remote from the isle. The island's meteorologist already employs a combination of electronic recording, computer analysis and telephone transmission via a modem; by using similar systems it would be possible to undertake, for example, accounting work, data analyses, or the preparation of typescripts. But such work may not appeal to those likely to be drawn to island life, and for life on Fair Isle to be attractive enough to keep people there it must clearly provide a satisfying means of earning a living, as well as an acceptable standard of amenities.

To live happily on a small island makes more demands on the individual than does life elsewhere. In addition to being much more dependent upon his — or her — own resources than those living in or near a larger community, the island dweller is also much more dependent upon his neighbours. Tolerance, adaptability and a willingness to co-operate are consequently among the most important of the qualities needed in island residents, and they are needed in women as well as men. Some of the families who have abandoned attempts to settle on Fair Isle did so because of ill-health, but others have left because one or

Unlike the earlier example, this 1986 wedding group includes many people —
among them the bride — from outwith Fair Isle. The young couple croft at
Vaasetter and there was much rejoicing when they added a baby girl to the
population in 1988. With young folk like these keen to rear families on the isle
the future for this small community looks much more promising today than it
did 30 years ago.

other of the partners was unable to integrate into the island community
or to accept the somewhat restricted social life. In the light of past
experience, the island Management Plan now recommends that every
effort should be made to encourage young Fair Islanders to remain on, or
return to, the island — and that other would-be residents should visit the
isle during the winter so that they can fully appreciate the harshness of
the climate before committing themselves. But with a growing number of

island-reared young people keen to return, after completing their education and perhaps working for a few years elsewhere, the prospect of maintaining a viable community can only be improving.

In 1956, when the deliberations of the Fair Isle Conference and the suggestions arising from it were being widely aired in the press, there were some who regarded the proposals for supporting the island as wishful thinking. One well-known journalist and author dismissed them thus: 'The endeavours of the NTS to attract to the Isle new crofting tenants are well meant but unrealistic. The depopulation of such localities is not due nowadays to economic causes — it is primarily psychological and sociological.' Time has fortunately proved him wrong; there now seems every reason to anticipate that the attractions of life on this rocky little island will continue to exert a sufficiently powerful pull to ensure that it remains inhabited. And, hopefully, visitors will continue to come in order to experience island life at first hand and to enjoy the spectacular scenery and wealth of wildlife. For Fair Isle's future as part of Scotland's living heritage seems likely to be dependent upon both the continuing enthusiasm of its small resident population and the continuing interest and goodwill of its many visitors.

Further Reading

There are many mentions of Fair Isle in books about Shetland, but only the few publications listed below are concerned solely, or mainly, with the island itself — and some of these are out of print. Much of the information included in this book was drawn from George Waterston's collection of abstracts and newscuttings, which is now on Fair Isle. A comprehensive bibliography of Fair Isle references (up to 1988) has been deposited in the libraries at Fair Isle Lodge & Bird Observatory, the Scottish Ornithologists' Club, and the George Waterston Memorial Centre.

Anon. (1986) Fair Isle National Scenic Area. Council of Europe, Strasbourg.

Bedford, Mary Duchess of (1938) A Bird-Watcher's Diary. (Privately printed).

Best, Betty (1987) A to P. An old record of Fair Isle words with phonetics (Booklet)

Eunson, Jerry (nd) The Shipwrecks of Fair Isle. (Booklet)

Eunson, Jerry (1961) The Fair Isle Fishing-Marks. Reprint from Scot. Studies. vol. 5 (2) 181 – 198.

Eunson, Jerry (1976) Words, Phrases and Recollections from Fair Isle. (Booklet)

Fair Isle Bird Observatory Trust Reports (1948 – 1988).

Fair Isle School 1878 – 1978. (1978) Commemorative booklet.

Holloway, John (1984) Fair Isle's Garden Birds. Shetland Times Bookshop, Lerwick.

Scott, Walter (1971) A check-list of the Flora of Fair Isle. Reprint from Fair Isle Bird Observatory Report 1971.

Stout, Cathy & Best, Betty (1988) Fair Isle. National Trust for Scotland, Edinburgh.

Waterston, George & Jones, Jean (1983) Fair Isle: a photographic history. Blackwood, Edinburgh.

Williamson, Kenneth (1965) Fair Isle and its birds. Oliver & Boyd, Edinburgh.

Index